Tasting
the
Word
of
God

Megan McKenna

Tasting the Word of God

Commentaries on the Sunday Lectionary

New City Press
Hyde Park, New York

Published in the United States by New City Press
202 Comforter Blvd., Hyde Park, NY 12538
www.newcitypress.com
©2010 Megan McKenna

Cover design by Durva Correia

Library of Congress Cataloging-in-Publication Data:

McKenna, Megan.
  Tasting the Word of God / by Megan McKenna.
    p. cm.
  Includes bibliographical references.
  ISBN 978-1-56548-355-2 (v.1 : pbk. : alk. paper) — ISBN 978-1-56548-356-9
(v.2 : pbk. : alk. paper) 1. Church year meditations. 2. Catholic Church—
Prayers and devotions. 3. Bible—Meditations. 4. Catholic Church. Lectionary
for Mass (U.S.). 5. Common lectionary (1992) I. Title.
  BX2170.C55M425 2010
  242'.3—dc22   2010025965

Printed in the United States of America

CONTENTS

Reflections:
Proper of Seasons and
Ordinary Time

SOLEMNITIES OF THE LORD DURING ORDINARY TIME

FEASTS OF THE LORD AND SAINTS

INTRODUCTION

In the sacred books the Father who is in heaven meets his children with great love and speaks with them; and the force in the Word of God is so great that it remains the support and energy of the Church, the strength of faith for her children, the food of the soul, the pure and perennial source of spiritual life. DIVINE REVELATION, Vatican II, #21

These words can serve as a vital foundation for this volume of commentaries on the Sunday Lectionary readings for the three year cycle of the Church's liturgy, worship, prayer and preaching. The Sunday readings serve to help us realize our connection to the universal Church praying as the Body of Christ together with one heart, mind, soul and body. The Sunday liturgy of Word and Eucharist is like a huge web strung across the world, holding it together and gathering all peoples into one before God. There is a Native American proverb which reads: God is a spider that weaves a web that holds the world together. The liturgy which is the work of the people of God, with God, for God and given over to God strengthens that web and draws all peoples ever more deeply into the presence of God and makes us ever more truly aware of our place with all of creation within the Trinity.

The Sunday readings take us through the great myth that lies at the core of our religion: the Paschal Mystery of the Incarnation, life, death and Resurrection of Jesus and Jesus' gift of his Spirit to all the world and the Church. A myth is a story so layered and powerful that it cannot just be told—it must be lived out with others, experienced, ritualized and celebrated as a life-long engagement and covenant. We are meant to become this mystery that we believe in and stake our lives upon as Christians, the beloved children of God the Father, with Jesus in the power of the Spirit.

The quote from the decree on DIVINE REVELATION reminds us of a number of points that are essential for us to remember and to both absorb internally and to put into practice, primarily with others. Our readings come from sacred books—books made holy by those who take them to heart and seek to put them into practice, and by the Spirit that inspired the authors to write them in response to the needs of the community of believers. In the Word of God we are met by our Father in love and we experience a dialogue—God speaking with us and all of us called to listen and respond. The readings are a place of community expression and communication that is threefold: God with us; us with God; and among ourselves in the listening presence of God.

And the relationship is that of Father and children, children of the same family, siblings, brothers and sisters of faith, who live in the freedom of the children of God, born of the same Spirit and belonging to the same body—the Body of Christ. In this Word, it is Jesus who speaks and prays with us to Father, with the Spirit knitting us together in body and soul. In the Sunday readings we are summoned and commanded to be what we have been called to be and initiated into—the heart of Christ in the world, the presence of the Risen Lord as Church in the world and the spirit of God in the world—all revealing the reality of God as Father and announcing this good news to the glory of God the Father, with Jesus, by the power of the Spirit.

This Word of God is a force so great, we are told that it remains the support and energy of the Church—it dwells with us as the foundation of our belief and the source of our lives and it is the very substance of our life—the breath and air that we breathe and need continually, as we do air to live and develop as mature believers and Christians that are known to be not only believers and disciples of Christ but the presence of the Risen Lord bringing hope, light and truth to others, and by our lives inviting them to become closer to dwelling within the Way, the Truth and the Life of Christ, found primarily in the Word of God and in those who are God's hands, hearts, minds, feet, soul and embrace in history today. The Word of God is the very lungs of the Church allowing us all to breathe, to live and to speak God's dreams and hopes for all creation and all God's children.

We are told that this Word of God is our strength of faith and the food of our souls and the perennial source of our spiritual life. In our liturgies we hear the Word proclaimed to those gathered; to sing the Word together in praise of God; we listen to the Word in stillness and reflection; we connect the Word of God to our own experiences and that of the Church in the world and to the politics, economics, and lives of all in the world, learning how to be Words of the Good News of God, of the Truth of God in Jesus Christ, of compassion for the poor and justice for all, calling all to reconciliation, the work of peace and abiding community where all are respected and given the dignity they deserve as the beloved children of God. [the proclamation of the readings, the responsorial psalms and acclamations, and the preaching of the Word and in dialog within the community] We live on the Word of God and need to chew on the Word, and ingest it and digest it as surely as we live on food and drink to sustain our bodies. We are told in the Word itself: *"One does not live by bread alone, but by every word that comes forth from the mouth of God."* (Mt 4:4; Dt 8:3)

In a sense the Sunday liturgy, and the Sunday readings are the main meals of our lives shared together, as we live through the seasons of the Paschal mystery—Advent, Christmas and Epiphany, the seven weeks of waiting for the Light, the Truth and the Peace of God in Christ to break into our world and The Word to leap down and take root in our bodies and lives as once The Word leapt down into the waiting flesh of Mary, becoming human in the mystery of the Incarnation. We seek to absorb this mystery of the Word made flesh, and the Light within us now as we seek to share that Light with all creation and all peoples of the world—being Epiphanies, moments of revelation and showing forth of the Light of Christ in the season called Ordinary Time. This season which is usually very short, bridges the season of the birth of the Word with the second season that marks the weeks of Lent and the passion that culminates in the source and heart of our hope and belief: the raising of Jesus from the dead by the Father in the love and power of the Spirit—

another seven weeks where we together as the Body of Christ seek to know in our own flesh and histories the passionate devotion and obedience to God, submitting our lives with Jesus to the glory and honor of God in the world.

This central feast of the Resurrection is the fulcrum that all the other seasons and readings either lead up or, or lead away from— for our resurrections begin in baptism that is celebrated at the Easter Vigil the apex of our liturgies all year. And in the next season, the seven weeks of Easter we seek to know the presence of the Risen Lord in the Church, in our communities, loose in the world and as Lord of all time and places. We hear over and over again of the birth of the Church, the gifting of the Spirit and how to recognize the Spirit among us and become filled with this presence of the Risen Lord as witness and testimony to God dwelling among us here and now. We are drawn in the Word of God to celebrate the Eucharist, the Body of Christ and become what we are, and what we share together in eating and drinking of the bread and wine, the Body and Blood of Christ. But we listen to how the Spirit abided in the early believing communities and is still at work, in power, in sacrament, in people, in the Church and in the world now, continuing the work of Christ today.

And last we hear the Word of God weekly through the season of ordinary time—a breathing period where we try once again, in each year to absorb all the deep mysteries we have heard proclaimed, profess to believe in and stake our lives upon, and incorporate into our own bodies and in our practice as the community that is the Body of Christ, the Church—the Sacrament of the Risen Lord in history today. It is almost half a year—there is so much to hear, to take heart from, to call us again to conversion and change, to rely on in hope, to call one another to forgiveness and reconciliation and freedom in the work for justice, the care of the poor, the making of peace and the ever deepening knowledge of the Truth of God in Jesus and the Spirit that is contained in the inspired readings of the Word of God. This is the time and the stories of Jesus' life and so, what is to become our own lives.

There are many commentaries on the readings of the Lectionary, some lengthy, others short bursts of insight, layered meanings and singular pieces of wisdom distilled from research, study, the sharing of scripture in small groups that call us to conversion of life and deepening of our personal spiritualities and our life together as the Body of Christ seeking to be that powerful presence in the world. In a sense there cannot be enough of these commentaries and reflections on the Word of God for no matter how many years we listen and celebrate the liturgies of the Church's year and participate in the great mysteries of our God: Father, Word and Spirit there is always so much more to say, more food for thought, more hope and courage distilled, more essence of the scent of God among us; more to hear of wonder, delight and the love that God bears for us in Jesus and the Spirit.

These are offered as jumping off places—as bits of food from others—as pieces of wisdom shared by other communities around the world, the poor, migrants, indigenous peoples, those struggling to live their faith where they are considered minorities and outsiders to the dominant culture or those who just share in common devotion to the Word of God and have fed on its richness over the years. Always read THE WORD first and let it sit in your soul, together with others. Let it seep into your own bones and spirit and share it around like warm bread and good wine and conversation. Then perhaps share these commentaries as gifts from others whose experience and faith can bring hope, insight and understanding, a thought that is new and provoking, a word that calls to conversion and says one more small thing about the Truth of the Word of God that was given to others. Let these commentaries remind you of the wider universal Church that feasts on the Word of God, where they have met the Father in love and where they speak back and speak to you in gratitude for the abundance and the depth of The Word made flesh dwelling among us in the Word of Scripture. This Word of God in these holy books are meant to be read so often that eventually we know whole pieces of them by heart and our own bodies become a piece of its good news to the poor.

- Megan McKenna

PROPER OF SEASONS
AND
ORDINARY TIME

SEASON OF ADVENT

A FIRST SUNDAY OF ADVENT

FIRST READING	Isaiah 2:1–5
Responsorial Psalm	Psalm 122:1–2, 3–4, 4–5, 6–7, 8–9
SECOND READING	Romans 13:11–14
GOSPEL	Matthew 24:37–44

✺ Now we begin the year of the Lord, with the prophecies of Isaiah whose visions are ones of justice, peace, light and freedom, hope for all the nations and unity among all peoples. This is the intent, the will of God for all on earth. God wants all to know wisdom and hear the Word of God, and walk in the paths of truth and communion. And there is to be no war, no aggression, no conflicts between nations and no preparation for killing. We are to be about the work of God: feeding the hungry, giving wisdom to all and living in the peace and light of God. This is what God is about—is this what we are about?

If not, wake up! Stop all the evil that leads to war, to killing, hate and divisions! Stop doing deeds that are laced with evil. It is time to stand in the light—the Light of the World that is Jesus the Son of Man coming to call us all to justice, to the truth. It is time to be seen for who we are and what we have done, individually and with others, in this world, in our times. There is no more time for preparation—Our God, the Son of Man is coming—NOW! Today is the day of the Lord.

B FIRST SUNDAY OF ADVENT

FIRST READING	Isaiah 63:16b–17, 19b; 64:2–7
Responsorial Psalm	Psalm 80:2–3, 15–16, 18–19
SECOND READING	1 Corinthians 1:3–9
GOSPEL	Mark 13:33–37

✺ Watch out! Stay awake! It is the ancient call to be attuned to the presence of God. We are doorkeepers, servants in charge and waiting on edge for the return of our Master. Evening, midnight, cock crow or dawn we could find ourselves standing before our God and called to account for our lives and actions. Our God is coming! It is Advent, and our God is always coming towards us, beckoning, bidding us to care about the household, the reign of God's peace with abiding justice in the world. We begin the year of the Lord 2006—will this year truly belong to God? Will we bear the name of the Holy One, our Father, our Redeemer so that all know that this year will serve to make holy the world?

C   FIRST SUNDAY OF ADVENT

FIRST READING	Jeremiah 33:14–16
Responsorial Psalm	Psalm 25:4–5, 8–9, 10, 14
SECOND READING	1 Thessalonians 3:12–4:2
GOSPEL	Luke 21:25–28, 34–36

The day of Justice is coming. This is God's justice, the only kind that brings security. This is God's promise. Paul's prayer for his people is that they increase and overflow with love for one another, blameless and holy until God comes. When will God come? When will the promise be reality? There will be signs but when the Son of Man comes we must stand up straight, knowing this is our ransom. Until then prayer, attentiveness and obedience to God is the only thing we are exhorted to cling to, together. Advent is for practicing—standing for the Son of Man, God's justice coming upon us.

A   SECOND SUNDAY OF ADVENT

FIRST READING	Isaiah 11:1–10
Responsorial Psalm	Psalm 72:1–2, 7–8, 12–13, 17
SECOND READING	Romans 15:4–9
GOSPEL	Matthew 3:1–12

We both look towards the coming of the child who will bring justice and peace—the child who will guide all nations to communion and care for the afflicted of each land. There will be truth and all will know that the Spirit of the Lord rests on him and those who follow him. And yet we look backwards for this child is grown to be a man and is with us, with John the Baptist as his herald who cries out to us to be ready and prepare the way for the incarnation—his birth into our lives once again in Word, in Eucharist, in peace upon earth and justice for the poor. We have been baptized for conversion and in water and the spirit. We have been forgiven, blessed and made the children of God with his beloved child Jesus. Are we ready? What preparations have we made this new year of grace 2008? Will it belong more completely and truthfully to God? What evidence are we giving that we have reformed and that the Spirit of God now dwells in us, in wisdom and knowledge, fear of the Lord, the work of justice and peace-making?

All has been written for harmony so that we might dwell in peace and encourage one another with the Scriptures. Are we imitating this Child of God being servants to one another, especially the servants of the poor and the victims of injustice and war? Wake up!

B   SECOND SUNDAY OF ADVENT

FIRST READING	Isaiah 40:1–5, 9–11
Responsorial Psalm	Psalm 85:9–10, 11–12, 13–14
SECOND READING	2 Peter 3:8–14
GOSPEL	Mark 1:1–8

How does God come to us? This is how it begins—this news of Jesus Christ, Son of God. He comes in the tradition of the prophets Isaiah and the voice crying out in the desert: prepare the way; level his paths. And John the Baptizer comes calling for a baptism of repentance that leads to forgiveness. Preparation: find the way, level out injustices and make the way in peace, repent, forgive others and turn towards the One who comes with the power and Spirit of God.The hand of our God comes with the strength of one who comforts and sets free. God draws near us.

C   SECOND SUNDAY OF ADVENT

FIRST READING	Baruch 5:1–9
Responsorial Psalm	Psalm 126:1–2, 2–3, 4–5, 6
SECOND READING	Philippians 1:4–6, 8–11
GOSPEL	Luke 3:1–6

✤ We are summoned to rejoice and dress in the splendor of God's glory, wrapping ourselves in the cloak of justice and bearing the miter of God's eternal name. It is time to stand, gathered, rejoicing at the Word of the Holy One, for our God leads us home. We are embraced with the justice and mercy of God. Are we rich in the harvest of justice that we have shared in? John the Baptizer proclaims that the promise is coming among us now if only we can see—to be baptized, our eyes washed out with repentance. Are we listening to God's Word?

A   THIRD SUNDAY OF ADVENT

FIRST READING   Isaiah 35:1–6a, 10
Responsorial Psalm   Psalm 146:6–7, 8–9, 9–10
SECOND READING   James 5:7–10
GOSPEL   Matthew 11:2–11

✤ Are we letting God be our strength, our hope, our courage, our joy and our vindication? Our God comes to save us, to open our eyes to the truth, and our ears to the Word spoken among us and to set us dancing and singing. There is no place for mourning and sorrow—we are the glory and splendor of our God more surely than any tree or land. We must learn to wait, like the land waits for harvest. Our God comes, not perhaps as the people of the rapture keep harping, but our God comes, in peace, in freedom, in the poor, in those who speak the Word of God, in justice, in forgiveness and mercy. He comes to those who suffer, who are patient and forgiving and he comes like the prophets: with a word that sears and startles. John heard of Jesus and wondered. And his friends ask Jesus, "Are you the one to come?" Look around. We know if our God is with us by the signs: healing, openness, conversion, freedom, the outcast are welcomed home, people dead in despair and misery are given life, and the good news is preached to the poor of the world. It is Advent and when we hear the words of John and Jesus it is time for us to take up the cry and the announcement—and be the words of proclamation and the presence of Good News to the poor of the world that cry out for peace upon the earth. If we are the least we had best start making Jesus' words come true in our world and have the effect that John had in our day and place.

B   THIRD SUNDAY OF ADVENT

FIRST READING   Isaiah 61:1–2a, 10–11
Responsorial Psalm   Lk 1:46–48, 49–50, 53–54
SECOND READING   1 Thessalonians 5:16–24
GOSPEL   John 1:6–8, 19–28

A man came, sent from God. He came as a witness to introduce the Light. John testifies that he is not the Light he is the voice crying out in the wilderness: make straight the way of the Lord. And he knows and makes others aware that the Other is in their midst and they do not know him. He himself is not worthy to bend before him and untie his sandal straps. It is Advent and we are to witness and introduce the Light to the world: to cry out with our words, our presence, our decisions and work for reconciliation and justice that this Other is in our midst and most are not aware of his presence. We learn to see, perhaps by bending and serving those in our midst most in need, in the corporal works of justice and mercy. Do we know him as he stands among us?

C   THIRD SUNDAY OF ADVENT

FIRST READING   Zephaniah 3:14–18a
Responsorial Psalm   Is 12:2–3, 4, 5–6
SECOND READING   Philippians 4:4–7
GOSPEL   Luke 3:10–18

Rejoice, shout, sing, be glad, and exalt! We are released from judgment and God is in our midst. There is no reason to be discouraged. Our God is renewing us in love and singing over us! Can you hear? Rejoice! We are to share generously, trust, pray for others, and live in gratitude for God's peace stands guard over us. What are we supposed to do? Share food, clothing, shelter. Stop being greedy and stealing from others. Do no harm, no violence, no lying. Are we changing? Are we living with anticipation, our hearts wondering? And this is only preparation, water washing out our eyes. The Good News is yet to come!

A FOURTH SUNDAY OF ADVENT

FIRST READING	Isaiah 7:10–14
Responsorial Psalm	Psalm 24:1–2, 3–4, 5–6
SECOND READING	Romans 1:1–7
GOSPEL	Matthew 1:18–24

The sign of God will be given whether it is wanted or not. The child will be born and his name will be Emmanuel—God with us. God's will will be done on earth. The time approaches for it to happen again in us, as it did with Ahaz, as it did with Mary. We can choose to resist like Ahaz or to accept with Mary. We are told to listen! This is what was promised from of old and the Scriptures record—that the child is born of God and is the Son of God, who will live, die and be raised from the dead and is the holiness of God still among us. God came that we might learn obedience to the Word of God made flesh and belong—all of us—to God in Jesus Christ. We are greeted as the beloved of God, as was Mary and Joseph, John and Elizabeth, and Jesus, The Beloved Son of God made flesh.

We hear the story from Joseph the dreamer, the just man. We see his belief and obedience. He is a Jew, who eats/sleeps and loves the Scriptures. So when the angel quotes scripture he arises and takes Mary and the child to be born into his heart and his house, obedient to the Word of God proclaimed to him. He breaks with the earlier law that would have Mary and the child stoned to death, or humiliated, shamed and sent away for her to bear the child alone. God is coming. And God is careful of the least of his people, his own Son being born among them, and will die terribly among them. The time is close. Are we ready for the Word of God to be born in us?

B FOURTH SUNDAY OF ADVENT

FIRST READING	2 Samuel 7:1–5, 8b–12, 14a, 16
Responsorial Psalm	Psalm 89:2–3, 4–5, 27, 29
SECOND READING	Romans 16:25–27
GOSPEL	Luke 1:26–38

With a week before the birth we flip backwards in time to the moment of the Incarnation when Jesus is conceived in Mary. The Holy Spirit came upon her and the power of the Most High overshadowed her...and now the holy child to be born will be called Son of God. The birth moment draws near. This child was conceived in freedom, in obedience to the Word of God and that Word will soon become flesh in history. How is this to be for us this year? We must ask for the courage to obey and to bring forth the Word in our flesh.

C   FOURTH SUNDAY OF ADVENT

FIRST READING   Micah 5:1–4a
Responsorial Psalm   Psalm 80:2–3, 15–16, 18–19
SECOND READING   Hebrews 10:5–10
GOSPEL   Luke 1:39–45

Ah Bethlehem, the least will be the home of the One who will be ruler, who is from of old, who is the shepherd, the reconciler who will bring them home and let them remain secure. His name shall be peace! This is the one who will do the will of God. The only sacrifice God has ever wanted: obedience, given freely. And Mary goes in haste to Judah, greets Elizabeth and she is recognized in her greeting (of peace). The Spirit surges from the Word she bears upon Elizabeth and stirs John into kicking with life. Mary is blessed for trusting in the Lord's words to her. We are blessed in trusting God's words too—will the Word take on our flesh this year? Will we obey and give our bodies, with Jesus to God in sacrifice?

SEASON OF CHRISTMAS

A B C NATIVITY OF THE LORD
December 25

FIRST READING | Isaiah 52:7–10
Responsorial Psalm | Psalm 98:1, 2–3, 3–4, 5–6
SECOND READING | Hebrews 1:1–6
GOSPEL | John 1:1–18 (or 1:1–5, 9–14)

It is time to cry out, to announce the glad tidings: Our God is King. Our God has come to bring us joy and to see the restoration of all our lives, to comfort and redeem us. Our God now belongs to all the nations and his bare arm is for all. This is the power of God, the power of a newborn who is the Son of God made flesh, through whom he created the universe. He is the reflection of the Father's glory and he is the sustaining power of life for all in the Spirit. We are called to worship the Trinity as we stand before the crèche and wonder at our God among us. But we must be careful not to get caught up in the piety of the child, for this child is the grown man, beloved of God, the Word since the beginning, the light, the truth, God of God. This child/man/God, when he came, was rejected by his own. This child is the enduring love of God and we have been given a share in this fullness of God. This is the only God we have ever seen. This is Jesus revealing God. This is what it means to be human. God is incarnated as one of us—we now meet God in every human being, in the Word and in God's enduring Love/Eucharist/the Body of Christ—all humanity. The way we love one another is the way we love God. God is born in us today.

A child is born to us! But who is he really? He is, from the beginning before creation, the Word of God. And this child is light that darkness cannot overcome. And the world, and even his own don't know him or receive him. But to those who see this child will give the power to become the children of God with him. The Word is made our flesh and pitches his tent among us. God has come home to dwell with his creation, his children on earth. History has been penetrated to its core, its heart and we see God's glory—the glory of an only Son coming from the Father, full of truth and loving-kindness. Do we see this glory? Because of the Incarnation do we see God's glory on the face of every human being? Look in love!

W Raise a cry! Shout for joy! We can see our Lord directly before our eyes. Our God has come to comfort and redeem us. We behold our salvation. God now speaks to us clearly in the person, the body of Jesus, the Son who is the reflection of the Father's glory, who is the sustaining Word. From the beginning this Word is God, with God, in God and now this Word dwells with us in the world, flesh among us. We have all been given a share in his life, his light, his goodness and love. God has taken on our flesh humbly, loving us beyond description. Do we know this God among us? Do we love this God?

A HOLY FAMILY OF JESUS, MARY, AND JOSEPH

FIRST READING	Sirach 3:2-6, 12–14
Responsorial Psalm	Psalm 128:1–2, 3, 4–5
SECOND READING	Colossians 3:15a, 16a
GOSPEL	Matthew 2:13–15, 19–23

W We hear the old wisdom of a family: mother/father and children, in this case culturally, the son who treats his parents with respect and dignity as they age, caring for them. But this is a human family. We belong as God's chosen ones to the family of God that is the Trinity, that we are initiated into at our baptisms. We belong to the Body of Christ—those who hear the Word of God and practice it—becoming ever more holy and beloved of God. We must act as the brothers and sisters of God with Jesus; forgiving, bearing with one another—everyone, including enemies; and loving all in all the practical ways that are demanded: humility, meekness (no violence) mercy, patience. We must dwell in peace and let the Word of God dwell with us (not just as individuals but as the community, the disciples and the company of Jesus—church). We are to live with joy and worship and do all to serve God's will and kingdom. Our duty—whether we are married, single, children, parents, grandparents, kin or the friends of God—is to be submissive to the Gospel and obey the Word of the Lord.

Being the family of God can be hard. It is fraught with violence, fleeing from evil and destruction as we try to save one another's lives, living with the ignorance of others (the magi who go to Herod), surviving in poverty and history (occupied territory of the Romans). But it is the Word of God in the Scriptures that tells us what to do and how to live with grace in all situations. We must listen and obey.

B HOLY FAMILY OF JESUS, MARY, AND JOSEPH

FIRST READING   Gen 15:1–6; 21:1–3
Responsorial Psalm   Psalm 105:1–2, 3–4, 5–6, 8–9
SECOND READING   Heb 11:8, 11–12, 17–19
GOSPEL   Luke 2:22–40 (or Luke 2:22, 39–40)

This is the Holy Family: Jesus, Mary, and Joseph, Simeon and Anna—all those who are kin in the Spirit, those called the anawim, the poor ones who live on hope and wait for the coming of God's power into the world. They are faithful and enduring, attentive and prayerful. They fulfill the law and yet live on the Spirit. And the model is Jesus himself who grows in stature and strength with wisdom and grace—through obedience to the law and Scriptures. How are we growing? In wisdom and grace, kin to all those who obey the will of God for life for all? Have we learned to recognize those who are born in grace and dwell together in the family of God?

C HOLY FAMILY OF JESUS, MARY, AND JOSEPH

FIRST READING   1 Samuel 1:20–22, 24–28
Responsorial Psalm   Psalm 84:2–3, 5–6, 9–10
SECOND READING   1 John 3:1–2, 21–24
GOSPEL   Luke 2:41–52

Hannah prays for a child and when God grants her that gift, she rejoices and returns the child to God when he is old enough to be weaned. The child has always belonged to Yahweh. Every child has from the beginning belonged to God and is entrusted to their parents to give back to God. We are first the children of God, conceived and birthed in love, in the Spirit of Jesus, the Word made flesh. This is who we truly are! We were created to love, each in our own singular way. Mary and Joseph had to learn that their child was not theirs, but belonged to God alone. We must spend this year searching for who Jesus truly is—not what we want him to be for us, but what he is before God. And we must, with Jesus, grow in wisdom and grace as we grow in years.

A B C   SOLEMNITY OF MARY, MOTHER OF GOD
January 1

FIRST READING	Numbers 6:22–27
Responsorial Psalm	Psalm 67:2–3, 5, 6, 8
SECOND READING	Galatians 4:4–7
GOSPEL	Luke 2:16–21

Time is relentless. Yet our times and our places are found to be holy in the wisdom and embrace of God. We have had God's blessings upon our lives always, but even more so with the coming of God as a human person into the world. Now we are God's beloved children with spirits that seek the face of our Father.

We have been given the hope once given to the shepherds and it is our time to go in haste to see and to understand what we have been told and to tell what we have heard. With Mary and Joseph we reflect upon all these things in our hearts. Treasuring and pondering all that others share with us about this Child, is the way we begin and the way of grace for the year 2007. We ponder the Gospel together.

Today we ponder Mary as the Mother of God and the gospel gives us one line that says volumes about her as a believer and mother of a child who is the Word Made Flesh among us and our God. "As for Mary, she treasured all these messages and continually pondered over them." Mary is a theologian, one who prays, treasuring and cherishing all that others have to say about this child and ponders, struggling to understand what their words might mean for her and as his parents and for her people and nation, Israel.

We find Mary, with Joseph and the child, lying in the manger. These are the poor of the earth, the child in a feeding trough for animals who is food, justice, hope and good news for the poor and the downtrodden, heavily burdened people of the earth. If we were to be situated in relation to a few people, where would we be found? And if we were to proclaim this God who is mothered by a poor woman what words would we ponder and pass on to those awaiting a message of hope?

✴ Jesus is born! Jesus' birth has made us all the beloved children of God, giving us God's own spirit so that we can call God "Abba" with Jesus. We now belong to God with the power of God as our own heritage. This power is given to bless and bring peace, to make the way of truth known to all and guide others to the worship of the Lord. With the shepherds we go to see and find this child, lying in poverty like so many of the earth and proclaim: every human being is cherished by God and called to help in saving the world. Today we face forward into the new year, with the blessings of God upon us. We must go in haste and share the blessing.

A B C   EPIPHANY OF THE LORD

FIRST READING   Isaiah 60:1–6
Responsorial Psalm   Psalm 72:1–2, 7–8, 10–11, 12–13
SECOND READING   Ephesians 3:2–3a, 5–6
GOSPEL   Matthew 2:1–12

✴ Light bursts forth upon us, and shatters the world's darkness. We live in radiance and our Lord shines over us. Now nations are to walk by his light—our light! Raise your eyes and look about and see all those who seek to gather and come. God desires to be known by everyone. All seek to praise God, to bring gifts to honor God's Holy One. We must live in this light, with all once called Gentiles now our brothers and sisters in God, members of the same body through the preaching of the Gospel. God is shown forth, made manifest in the light that radiates from our lives, our words and our welcome of others.

It is the ancient familiar story of 3 outsiders who saw in the sky the portent of God's entering humankind and dwelling upon the earth. They journey and meet Herod who seeks to harm the child they seek and they give him what he needs to kill the children in his search for Emmanual, God-with-us. Only when they see the Child, do they know wisdom and return by another route. We too seek but have we found the wisdom of the Child who is profound peace, the savior of the poor?

Epiphany means manifestation or showing forth. Here, outsiders discover the revelation of the mystery of God as a human child born among us. This child belongs to the world and will shepherd his people Israel, but reign over the whole peoples in forgiveness, justice and mercy. Those from afar off strangers see what those who are inside a religious tradition cannot perceive. Sadly even the teachers and priests who know the promises that were meant to sustain the people under oppression live in collusion with their rulers who see these prophets' words as threatening to their own power.

Epiphany is about power and what power we worship. There is the power of the Word of God that sustains. There is the power of Herod and nations that only serves its own ends. There is the power of the Child of the Star who comes to liberate and free. There is the power of worship and pilgrimage in search of the truth. There is the power of dreams that protect others. What powers do we serve?

The Light has come! God's glory dwells among us. Do we have our eyes lifted to the radiance, standing with others who have sought the light? The wise men sought the night sky and the stars for indicators of where to look for the new power born on earth. We have been told to look in the Word of God, among the poor, and with the prophets who cry for justice. We are not to look to leaders in the world, but in the cries and hopes of those who wait for God's presence in justice. They came and gave their gifts, worshipped and went home another way. We stand always in the presence of the Light of Truth and the Bread of Mercy. What are we giving to others as worship of God and do we go home by his Way?

A BAPTISM OF THE LORD

FIRST READING   Isaiah 42:1–4, 6–7
Responsorial Psalm   Psalm 29:1–2, 3–4, 3, 9–10
SECOND READING   Acts 10:34–38
GOSPEL   Mt 3:13–17

Jesus is baptized and sees the Spirit of God come down to rest upon him. And he hears the voice confirming who he is: "This is my Son, the Beloved; he is my Chosen One." Today we remember our baptisms and are reconfirmed in who we are called to be. Our Father says to each of us: "This is my Son, my Daughter, the Beloved; you are my Chosen Ones." By baptism each of us is given the same relationship to God our Father, in the power of the Spirit that Jesus himself knew with God. We stand together as brothers and sisters with Jesus and as the beloved children of God. Now our God depends on us, and looks to us to be the presence of truth and love in the world.

B BAPTISM OF THE LORD

FIRST READING   Isaiah 55:1–11
Responsorial Psalm   Is 12:2–3, 4bcd, 5–6
SECOND READING   1 Jn 5:1–9
GOSPEL   Mark 1:7–11

The water is here! Come to the feast of the poor and incline your ear so that your soul might live! See—there is one whose thoughts and ways are not like ours, but like our God's. God's ways are those of forgiveness, mercy and giving, giving of seed, water, bread, nourishment and obedience. This one is God's beloved, his chosen son. And in this generosity of God, in Jesus' baptism we are made his own beloved, his chosen ones too. We are made to be forgiving, merciful and giving, obeying God with Jesus and living in God's rich and satisfying Spirit. Do we live in this freedom of the children of God?

C BAPTISM OF THE LORD

FIRST READING — Isaiah 40:1—5, 9–11

Responsorial Psalm — Psalm 104:1b–2, 3–4, 24–25, 27–28, 29–30

SECOND READING — Tit 2:11–14; 3:4–7

GOSPEL — Lk 3:15–16, 21–22

✺ Be comforted, my people! We are released from bondage, freed! Look even the earth responds to this voice: valleys raised up, mountains brought low, the way smoothed out, and glory everywhere. Now we cry out, "Here is your God!" He is shepherd, tender with the young, a leader who carries his own. God comes so close, and is so human among us.

"By baptism," we are now made holy in God. We are saved by the mercy of God, that is the person of Jesus come into our world and he seeks to purify us and make us holy as he is holy. The people wait in anticipation—do we? Do we live with the fire and Spirit of our baptisms? Jesus was praying; the Spirit came upon him and the Father declares, "You are my Son, this day I have begotten you." Today we too are begotten of God and the Father declares: "You are my daughter, my son."

A B C FEAST OF STO. NIÑO

FIRST READING — Isaiah 9:1–7

Responsorial Psalm — Psalm 97:1, 2–3, 3–4, 5–6

SECOND READING — Eph 1:3–6, 15–18

GOSPEL — Mt 18:1–5, 10 (or Lk 2:41–52)

✺ Whose heart is not moved by the birth of a child? Who can experience the happy face of a child and not feel a surge of hope? Hundreds of years before Christ was born, the meaning of his coming was described: "a light has dawned on those who live in the land of the shadow of death...for a child is born to us." This feast of Sto. Niño is special to those whose hopes are awakened by children, who see in the child God who brings love, peace, and security. The birth of each child is a sign that God has not yet given up on the human race. Sto. Niño, teach us to trust as you did in God, your Father, our Father.

✳ What child is this? This child is light dawning in the darkness of death. This child is joy in freedom from bondage. This child is peace in being liberated from war and destruction. This child is Wonderful Counselor, Everlasting Father, Prince of Peace. This child is mighty God. And this child makes us look differently at every human person as a child of God. In Jesus' time a child was not just a young human being under the age of 12, it was anyone who was without power, without recourse, slaves, outsiders/strangers, the sick, the shunned, the sinner, the poor and it is they who swarm to the presence of Jesus the beloved Child of God. The kingdom belongs to them first and unless we become like them, needing, having no power but God's and reveling in the presence of God we will not know either God or the kingdom among us.

✳ This child is light in darkness; joy as at harvest times, freedom from poverty, misery and bondage; the end of war and violence. He is peace, forever, his dominion vast and established on justice. And we are the sons and daughters of the Father of Jesus, chosen with Jesus since the creation of the world to be holy and live in his presence.

Mk We are to be children like this one who blesses the world with light, joy and freedom—this is what we are to become like, in imitation and in following the One who is peace with justice forever for those most in need.

Mt We are to be the children who are greatest before God by serving as the least among our brothers and sisters, in imitation of Jesus, his beloved child who was lowly and the servant of all. We are to receive the children: the least of the world, the forgotten, poor and without power with the gentleness of God in Jesus.

Lk We must be the children of God, about our Father's business first, knowing the Father and worshipping with Jesus. We must be subject to those around us, obedient but also faithful to God first and foremost. And we must ponder all these words and works of Jesus so that we might become the children of light, the peacemakers of God.

SEASON OF LENT

A   FIRST SUNDAY OF LENT

FIRST READING   Genesis 2:7–9; 3:1–7
Responsorial Psalm   Psalm 51:3–4, 5–6, 12–13, 17
SECOND READING   Romans 5:12–19
GOSPEL   Matthew 4:1–11

We have been made and live by the very breath of God and we are born with freedom of choice: we can choose life like God, or we can choose what leads to death and turn from God. It has been so from the beginning. We begin Lent knowing we must choose: to live in the freedom of the children of God, as we vowed at our baptisms, strengthened by the Word and will of God or we can choose to take care of ourselves first and foremost, make it according to the powers and evil rife in the world around us that hinders us all from living as God's children. And we can even use religion to protect us from becoming what we were born to be, using our relationship with God to fend off suffering and death which is part of being mortal, created by God or we can obey the Word of God, with Jesus, accepting and making holy even suffering and death, trusting that our God is the God of life who will be with us through all things. Father, give us your Spirit in the Word of Scripture so that we might obey, with Jesus and live our lives in your freedom of grace and truth, bringing your kingdom of justice and peace into our world. May this year 2005 be one of your grace and truth, not dominated by injustice, cruelty and what hinders your beloved children from your life.

B   FIRST SUNDAY OF LENT

FIRST READING   Genesis 9:8–15
Responsorial Psalm   Psalm 25:4–5, 6–7,8–9
SECOND READING   1 Peter 3:18–22
GOSPEL   Mark 1:12–15

On this first Sunday of Lent we hear of water and the ark that saved creation and all that was made from the flood. We also hear of the bow in the clouds that signals the new creation and covenant of God with all that He created. Never again will waters destroy the earth. And Peter reminds us that Noah and a few persons escaped—now we escape through the waters of baptism! It too is a covenant with God, and a promise to live with a clear conscience through the resurrection of Jesus. We live now, with Jesus, or as the rite says: We live now, hidden with Christ in God, held in the Spirit's grasp, resisting evil and being the good news of God for all.

C FIRST SUNDAY OF LENT

FIRST READING — Deuteronomy 26:4–10
Responsorial Psalm — Psalm 91:1–2, 10–11, 12–13, 14–15
SECOND READING — Romans 10:8–13
GOSPEL — Luke 4:1–13

Together we gather and collect the fruits of our belief and lives and come before the altar of the Lord, giving over to God the only gift of worship that God demands—us, our lives and relationships, our bodies and souls, our incomes and our remaking of the world and all that has been made. And we rejoice that we are God's people and dwell in his presence. We gather, all of us, rich in diversity, of nations, peoples, languages, races. And what binds us as one is the Word of God that is in our hearts, on our lips and proclaimed to us daily. We are saved, and now it is up to us to live in gratitude and imitation of our crucified and risen Lord.

Jesus is tempted and we are tempted. We are confronted with Satan, the Hinderer in all the areas of our lives: income, security, daily needs and the use of the world's resources. We must resist the powers and the glory of the kingdoms of the world: military, prestige, selfish wealth, greed/avarice of resources and people, economic and political injustices, lies, lack of responsibility for choices. And we must refuse to be mastered by any sin: self-righteousness, thinking we're ok, we're trying and it is others who are the problem, that if we do outward religious works we will be protected from harm. It is time to face the reality that we must live on the Word, adore the Trinity alone and not test God, but bow in submission to God's will.

A   SECOND SUNDAY OF LENT

FIRST READING   Genesis 12:1–4a
Responsorial Psalm   Psalm 33:4–5, 18–19, 20, 22
SECOND READING   2 Timothy 1:8b–10
GOSPEL   Matthew 17:1–9

※ Abram obeys God, leaves everything: his country, his family, father's house, land and is made the nation that belongs to God. He is made a blessing and made covenant with God. We are summoned as a people to remember we belong to no country, land, family or household but we first and foremost belong to God—that is our blessing and our covenant that we are the beloved children in the universal family of the New Covenant Blessing in Jesus the Lord. Jesus calls his disciples to the cross and resurrection and they resist and so he calls them up the mountain to pray with him and see the Glory of God in his own Body so that they will come with him as followers of the Son of Man, leaving all, even their lives to belong to him and know resurrection life. We are brought to pray with Jesus, to be told to listen only to his Word, to see only Jesus and to believe in his glory, in spite of the suffering, violence and death all around us. Father, let us be true believers, leaving all to follow you through suffering and death into glory, knowing you are with us and that you are here to transfigure our lives and all of history with justice and peace. Amen.

B   SECOND SUNDAY OF LENT

FIRST READING   Genesis 22:1–2, 9a, 10–13, 15–18
Responsorial Psalm   Psalm 116:10, 15, 16–17, 18–19
SECOND READING   Romans 8:31b–34
GOSPEL   Mark 9:2–10

※ First there was the covenant with earth and the human race with Noah. Now there is the covenant between God and Abraham and the people. God wants everything from us, but God is the God of life and the future and so does not want our children or anyone else's children in sacrifice. What God wants is our obedience. We stand with Jesus who obeyed even in the face of others murdering him. And we are told to look to Jesus, the fullness of all the liberating law (Moses) and the prophets (Elijah) and stake our lives on Jesus' word alone, only on Jesus. And then we will walk with him all the way to the cross, and onto the glory of resurrection.

C   SECOND SUNDAY OF LENT

FIRST READING	Genesis 15:5–12, 17–18
Responsorial Psalm	Psalm 27:1, 7–8, 8–9, 13–14
SECOND READING	Philippians 3:17–4:1
GOSPEL	Luke 9:28b–36

Abram knows God in darkness, fire, birds of prey and in the words of promise that he will be a people like the stars and that this land will be their, as God's gift. As God's own Body, we know God much more intimately and personally. Abram obeys and does what God commands. We must obey and live as the citizens of heaven, not any nation on earth. We must not live as enemies of the cross of Christ—those set on things of the world: military, economic, and political power, selfishness, individuality, making it in their field, or living with greed, avarice, sloth, unfaithfulness. We must stand firm in Jesus.

Jesus shows us the God of light, the God of incarnation, God in his own flesh and body. As he prays, he is transfigured and we see God's glory shining through his very person—this is what we stake our lives on, and live in faith on. Jesus is seen as the new liberator and lawgiver, the new prophet. His mantle of justice is his own flesh and he will go to the cross and hand over his person and life. He invites us to come with him and to know both the burden of the cross and its glory in our lives. We are drawn into the Trinity and the Father tells us: "Listen to him!" And we must obey in the power of the Spirit. Who are we obeying and listening to this Lent?

A   THIRD SUNDAY OF LENT

FIRST READING	Exodus 17:3–7
Responsorial Psalm	Psalm 95:1–2, 6–7, 8–9
SECOND READING	Romans 5:1–2, 5–8
GOSPEL	John 4:5–15, 19b–26, 39a, 40–42

✹ The Sunday of water readings. The people thirst in the desert and cry out against God and Moses. Moses is commanded to strike the rock and bring forth water and he obeys and the people have water, even after testing God. And Jesus thirsts and a woman of Samaria comes to the well. She is questioned and led through the process of conversion, belief and knowledge of who Jesus is until she leaves her water jar at the well and goes home with the living water of the Word and Spirit within her. Yet she still needs the community of the Word and paschal mystery (the three days he spends with them) to get past her limited personal experience of him to come to know him as the Savior of the World How thirsty are we? For baptism, for the Word of God, for the truth, for knowledge of Jesus, for community, for our God who saves the whole world? Are we still testing God for our immediate concerns and oblivious to the Water of Life that is in our midst? Jesus, you thirst for us. Seize our hearts and lives so that we might come to worship our God in spirit and truth with you. Amen.

B THIRD SUNDAY OF LENT

FIRST READING   Ex 20:1–17 (or Ex 20:1–3, 7–8, 12–17)
Responsorial Psalm   Psalm 19:8, 9, 10, 11
SECOND READING   1 Cor 1:22–25
GOSPEL   John 2:13–25

✹ We return to our roots as a people, receiving the law together. This is our heritage and is meant to be the foundation of our ethics, morality and decisions. The first three are about God, the fourth is the bridge of our families and the last six have to do with society, our neighbors. The law is meant to bind us all together as one, in covenant with God. And as Christians we are further given the wisdom of the Cross that holds us together and binds us at our hearts at the place where our God and the rest of the world meets. Jesus is adamant that true worship of God is not ritualistic or liturgical but found in zeal for the honor of God in our lives. And Jesus knows our hearts as we come together to pray. What does he see in our hearts today?

C THIRD SUNDAY OF LENT

FIRST READING   Exodus 3:1–8a, 13–15
Responsorial Psalm   Psalm 103:1–2, 3–4, 6–7, 8, 11
SECOND READING   1 Corinthians 10:1–6, 10–12
GOSPEL   Luke 13:1–9

Moses the shepherd tending the flock is accosted by the burning bush and the voice of God. He hears of God's compassion and concern for his broken and afflicted people. God has come to rescue them—and he is sending Moses to them. Moses wants to know God's name. He is told: "I AM… This is my name forever." A strange name but this is the God of life, creation, history, ancestors, promise and calling, the God of faithful Word and presence with the people. They will learn.

We have known this God who gave manna and water and we know the God who has given us Jesus, bread and wine, eucharist, baptism and confirmation and the Word in Scripture and the Word made flesh among us, yet, do we know God, or like those who went before us, do we need to be questioned, "Is God pleased with us?" Jesus is telling us that if we don't repent NOW the day will come when it will be too late. Do we produce fruit (justice, virtue, faithfulness, forgiveness, etc.) or is there nothing to show in our lives again this year? One more chance: manure us, chop at our roots and hope. If not, cut the tree down so that it doesn't negatively effect everything around it. Choose!

A FOURTH SUNDAY OF LENT

FIRST READING   1 Samuel 16:1b, 6–7, 10–13a
Responsorial Psalm   Psalm 23:1–3a, 3b–4, 5, 6
SECOND READING   Ephesians 5:8–14
GOSPEL   John 9:1–41
                             (or Jn 9:1, 6–9, 13–17, 34–38)

Yahweh sees with the heart. And Yahweh's spirit takes over a person (like David) from the moment he is anointed. The blind man is anointed with Jesus' spit and when he washes in the pool, in obedience to Jesus' word, the Spirit begins to take him over. With each encounter, each confrontation he grows stronger and aligns himself more and more with the person of Jesus, until he is thrown out from the temple. Jesus finds him and reveals himself to him as the Son of Man, persecuted and rejected (as the blind man was because he stood up for Jesus). Lord, you see into our hearts—let your Spirit deepen in us and make us stand up for you and what you speak as the truth, the way and the life for all peoples. And may we know you as the Son of Man, crucified, risen from the dead and the Light, the judge of the world.

B FOURTH SUNDAY OF LENT

FIRST READING   2 Chronicles 36:14–16, 19–23
Responsorial Psalm   Psalm 137:1–2, 3, 4–5, 6
SECOND READING   Ephesians 2:4–10
GOSPEL   John 3:14–21

We hear the litany of infidelity, abomination of the nations, war, violence and pollution of the temple (worship in the midst of doing evil). And as they draw away from God, God tries with prophets, warnings, compassion, outsiders that attack them. But nothing brings them back, not even the destruction of the temple, and of Jerusalem; captivity and exile. And redemption comes from an outsider—Cyrus, King of Persia—who helps them go home.

It is Jesus who helps us go home. It is not our doing, but the gift of God. We are told to look up at the Son of Man crucified and see our deliverance and then to walk in the light and act in truth.

When will we learn as a people of God?

C FOURTH SUNDAY OF LENT

FIRST READING   Joshua 5:9a, 10–12
Responsorial Psalm   Psalm 34:2–3, 4–5, 6–7
SECOND READING   2 Corinthians 5:17–21
GOSPEL   Luke 15:1–3, 11–32

The people arrive in Canaan and when they celebrate Passover, the manna ceases. They are home and eat together of the unleavened cakes and parched grain. They celebrate God's removal of the reproach of Egypt's bondage and slavery. They are free. We too know this celebration, this forgiveness and reconciliation with God in the person of Jesus. We are to celebrate our coming home to God by being God's ambassadors and letting God appeal to others through us. We live now so that we might draw others into the presence and intimacy of God through our lives.

We hear the familiar story of the lost sons and the forgiving, loving, faithful father who waits on both of them. He waits for one to come back, no matter the reason and then forgives him, lavishes his love on him, and throws a party so that all might be a part of his joy. And he waits on the elder son, for him to recognize his love and understanding, though he knows that his son considers himself a slave in his own house, because he does not know his father. And he goes begging and pleading for him to come in and know the joy and life of forgiveness (from the father) and reconciliation (with his brother and father and everyone). Are we forgiving, reconciling, and joyful that our God has brought us all home in Jesus' life and death and resurrection?

A   FIFTH SUNDAY OF LENT

FIRST READING   Ezekiel 37:12–14
Responsorial Psalm   Psalm 130:1–2, 3–4, 5–6, 7–8
SECOND READING   Romans 8:8–11
GOSPEL   John 11:1–45
                          (or Jn 11:3–7, 17, 20–27, 33b–45)

The raising of beloved Lazarus from the dead so that his dying and rising can strengthen the faith of the disciples. Jesus returns to where they want to kill him and brings life—life that is different than just being brought back out of a tomb—life that is everlasting—Resurrection Life. This is the consummation of John's gospel—Jesus' statement: "I am the Resurrection and the Life; whoever believes in me, though he die, shall live. Whoever is alive by believing in me will never die. Do you believe this?" This is what every catechumen, each person approaching the waters of baptism, to be buried with Christ is asked. Do we believe? Do we stake our lives on Jesus' life, death and resurrection—standing down all that is of death, evil, sin, injustice and hate knowing that even if we die, our God will give us life? Lord, we are so close to walking towards the cross and death with you—help us to stake our lives on your life, your Word and your love of the Father. Call us by name and bring us out of death.

B   FIFTH SUNDAY OF LENT

FIRST READING   Jeremiah 31:31–34
Responsorial Psalm   Psalm 51:3–4, 12–13, 14–15
SECOND READING   Hebrews 5:7–9
GOSPEL   John 12:20–33

Always the hope of a new covenant, written on hearts, not stone this time, but flesh and blood. God will have his people and they will be able to know God intimately, from the least to the greatest. Jesus is this covenant, obedience itself, reverent, even in suffering. And it is outsiders who seek the presence of Jesus through Philip's intervention. Jesus proclaims that he, the Son of Man, just judge of the nations, the lamb of God will be lifted up, crucified and yet he will be raised in glory by the Father. He is the servant of God and we are to be God's servants. The hour of dying and rising approaches. We, with Jesus cannot avoid it. And in facing death, judgment comes upon the world, and Jesus will draw all to himself. It is time for us to be drawn to the cross together with Jesus.

C   FIFTH SUNDAY OF LENT

FIRST READING   Isaiah 43:16–21
Responsorial Psalm   Psalm 126:1–2, 2–3, 4–5, 6
SECOND READING   Philippians 3:8–14
GOSPEL   John 8:1–11

"See I am doing something new! Now it springs forth, do you not perceive it?" Isaiah sings of the freshness, the newness, the rampant life on the earth, even in deserts and among the animals. The Lord opens a way in every situation and brings waters of life to the chosen people to drink (these are the waters of baptism, a way into the tomb of death and a way of life that is unbelievably fresh). Paul tells us what this water is—it is the light of the surpassing knowledge of my Lord Jesus Christ and his power flowing from the resurrection. We too must wish to know Christ and this power, by sharing in his sufferings and being formed into the pattern of his death.

Jesus is brought a woman caught in adultery—it is a set-up to trap Jesus. They care nothing for the woman or the law or truth. They want Jesus to make a decision that will turn a group against him. If he chooses the law then he will lose the people. If he chooses mercy than the leaders and priests, etc. will have more information to use against him. But Jesus does a new thing. He makes a path in a crowd that seeks to kill and leaders that are inhuman and self-righteous and evil. He does nothing and refuses to choose one of their options. His choice is always the truth, and forgiveness and mercy—no matter the consequences. And us—where do we stand, with those quick to condemn others and make them pay publicly for what they did (not really caring about the law, but intent on going after people)? Or are we at least honest enough to know we stand with the woman, caught in our unfaithfulness, yet offered the protection and forgiveness of God?

A B C   PALM SUNDAY OF THE LORD'S PASSION

FIRST READING   Isaiah 50:4–7
Responsorial Psalm   Psalm 22:8–9, 17–18, 19–20, 23–24
SECOND READING   Philippians 2:6–11
GOSPEL   Matthew 26:14–27:66
                                     Mark 14:1—15:47
                                        Luke 23:1–49

The week of passion, of devotion, of suffering and death and life given over begins and we are summoned to choose by whose side we will walk. The choice: to be with or against the suffering servant of Yahweh, intent on bringing justice to the nations, speaking a word to sustain the weary, to listen and be a disciple, to suffer our share of the burden of the gospel and being the followers of Jesus and not despair in the face of violence, hate and injustice. Lord, may we walk in your shadow, intent on following you, even unto death. Teach us how to resist evil and 'set our faces like flint' trusting in your life and truth. May the passion of our lives belong to you alone and our very lives be the sacrifice day to day that does justice, forgives, speaks truly and cares for the broken and suffering of the world. Lord Jesus, may you find your friends at your side, walking the way to the cross and resurrection—this year.

It is time to face death with Jesus. Isaiah tells us how we are to endure: speak to the weary and rouse them, open our ears to the Word, to suffer and not turn back and to absorb the hate and pain that is inflicted on us. God is our help and we will not be disgraced though we may be killed. We are to set our faces like flint and hang onto God for a dearer life. We are bound with Christ in God, in suffering and death and in glory. We must all die, being human. And we must die as we have lived, faithful to God with Jesus the Word, not grasping at life but taking on the attitude of Christ who is the LORD of life. We worship by living and dying together with Jesus for the truth. The passion of Jesus is our Passion.

This is the week that we pick up our cross—our share of the burden of preaching the gospel—and walk with Jesus along the way to dying and rising with him. We are called to look at Jesus who acts as the one who speaks truthfully and suffers, enduring and calling out to God who is his help and trusting that God is with him in his suffering and dying. We must be as Christ, facing evil, the violence and injustice of the world and refusing to participate in it, or to live in collusion with it. We are to humbly obey the God of Life, resisting all evil/death as the Body of Christ, and seeking to comfort, to console, to accompany those who suffer, especially those who suffer because of injustice and others' insensitivity and hatred.

This is the week that we are called to draw near to the cross, to learn its wisdom and to understand the power of forgiveness and mercy that is the sign of our salvation and freedom. We vow to live under no sign of power but the sign of the cross—the sign of the Trinity, the sign of inclusion and hope in the face of death. Let us go with him, all the way to glory.

EASTER TRIDUUM

A B C   HOLY THURSDAY

FIRST READING   Exodus 12:1–8, 11–14
Responsorial Psalm   Psalm 116:12–13, 15–16bc, 17–18
SECOND READING   1 Corinthians 11:23–26
GOSPEL   John 13:1–15

This is the feast of friends and the feast of freedom shared. This intimacy and power is shared, not only in the bread and wine, the sacrifice and the meal, but more intimately even than this—in the washing of the disciples' feet. Jesus lays aside his garment (as he will lay down his life) and bends before his friends, washing their dirty worn feet—worn from traveling with him and following him on his way. This is the way of liberation, freedom and friendship for those who claim intimacy with God in Jesus. We are to bend before one another, washing one another's feet before we sit and eat of the feast of freedom, the bread and wine that is the Body and Blood of Jesus. We must touch the bodies of all those, (even Judas) with tender regard, washing, healing, soothing and being the servant of all, down on the floor with Jesus. This is holy. This is what friends do for each other. This is the unbelievable love of our God for us in Jesus and it is what makes us one, in communion.

Tonight the covenant is made whole again. We hear the ancient one of exodus—liberation from death and bondage, from slavery and Egypt—as we are called out as a people, sharing the lamb of God, with its blood smeared on the doorposts where they eat to their coming freedom. We remember. And we celebrate with the new Lamb of God, Jesus who will be taken out, crucified and will rise from the dead. We sit at table to break his bread and eat to our lives and deaths and resurrection with him, in him and through him. But first we wash feet—for that is the only memorial we are given in John. This is what is to be the perpetual institution: service of others, even those who betray us, service and love unto death. Then when we live this way, we share the feast with other sinners being saved and walk the death and resurrection with Jesus who washes our feet, and head and hands and hearts this night. We imitate and remember, and put it all back together again in love.

✷ This is the night of tenderness, of love, of touching and words of endearment. This is the night for remembering all that God has done for us from the beginning—exodus, Passover, freedom. This is the night that we are given a God who bends before us and washes our feet, knowing that each one of us betrays him, lacks love for him, thinks first of ourselves even as we claim to belong to him. This is the night that we are given an example of a life—in service and regard for one another, inclusion of all sinners at the table of the Lord, even feet cared for—as a way of imitating and becoming like our Lord. This is the night of friends brought near and friends parted. This is the night we are given the Body of Jesus, as a servant, as bread and wine, in a new covenant of love unto death. This is the night we are made one in God again so that together we might leave this place and together go with God to the cross and resurrection. This is the night we stand and proclaim the death of the Lord until he comes, knowing that God will raise him, and raise us all from the dead—in our baptisms and one day, in glory.

A B C   GOOD FRIDAY OF THE LORD'S PASSION

FIRST READING   Isaiah 52:13–53:12
Responsorial Psalm   Psalm 31:2, 6, 12–13, 15–16, 17, 25
SECOND READING   Hebrews 4:14–16, 5:7–9
GOSPEL   John 18:1—19:42

✷ This is what our God looks like, in human flesh like us, rejected, scorned, belittled, tortured, treated inhumanly, when others seek to destroy him and mar any resemblance he bears to a man. But our God knows what we do—to so many in every age and our God is Emmanuel, God with us, with us in suffering and death, with us in knowing the rage and hate that humans inflict on one another, with us as the victim of injustice, evil and sin—that is individual, in groups, legal under the law, self-righteous, vindictive, nationalistic, acceptable and inevitable. And in Jesus' terrible way to death, our God says NO! never again—do not kill anyone, ever, in any way for I am the God of life and I am deep in the heart and flesh of every human being. Whatever you do to each other, I take it you did it to my beloved son, my beloved daughter, to me, to my flesh. But this is the just servant who will know light and knowledge of God and bear and take away guilt. Jesus surrendered to death and intercedes for us still. This is what we are exhorted to do: surrender to death when it is time and to always intercede for one another, especially our enemies and to trust in God for life.

We begin with the description of the beloved child of God so marred that he no longer appears even human, so stricken and afflicted, harshly treated, maimed, tortured and despised because he was so human, so true God in flesh among us. We look upon our God who looks like us and see what we do to one another when we destroy what God has made in his own image and likeness. Today we must see that what we do to God incarnate is what we do to each other despising one another, making enemies out of the beloved children of God. Jesus in his flesh bore all the burdens/evil/sin/violence and injustice of the world, but we are called to fill up what is lacking in his sufferings and to stand with the crucified of the world—with Jesus—so to share in his glory. But today we must die and see the destruction of human beings that we all share in, and ask mercy for our sin against God and one another. We must die to what is not life. We must die in God.

The ancient and familiar readings of Isaiah—the description of the sufferings and death of the Servant-Son Beloved of God, his agony and his trust in God, crying out as he surrenders himself in death—need to be read slowly, letting them sink into our hearts and stirring us to admit our own sin and our part in the suffering of others and to look at the crucified one still in our midst because of our sin, our evil and injustice, our violence. Christ is in agony until the end of time. This day is good because in Jesus obedience we are saved. Jesus lives to honor his Father alone and submits to death, yet forgives those who murder him. This day is good only if we resolve to live with that same trust in the face of suffering, persecution for justice, for the sake of the kingdom and the Name, and learn forgiveness, trusting that Our Father is with us and Jesus' own Spirit is in our hearts and bodies.

Today we are invited to join the community of the beloved disciples who stand at the foot of the cross, a silent witness to justice, caring for those left without support or protection by injustice and violence. We are invited to stand in the shadow of the cross and to stand with all those who are murdered, violently, or executed legally, and especially those who are innocent. We are invited to stand together, the new family of Jesus the Crucified Lord and die to ourselves so as to live in the freedom of the children of God.

THE VIGIL IN THE HOLY NIGHT OF EASTER

A B C   HOLY SATURDAY

FIRST READING	Genesis 1:1—2:2
Responsorial Psalm	Psalm 104:1–2, 5–6, 10, 12, 13–14, 24, 35
SECOND READING	Genesis 22:1–18
GOSPEL	Matthew 28:1–10
	Mark 16:1–7
	Luke 24:1–12

FIRST READING	Genesis 1:1—2:2
Responsorial Psalm	Psalm 104:1–2, 5–6, 10, 12
	(or Psalm 33:4–5, 6–7, 12–13, 20–22 (3b)

SECOND READING	Genesis 22:1–18
Responsorial Psalm	Psalm 16:5, 8, 9–10, 11

THIRD READING	Exodus 14:15—15:1
Responsorial Psalm	Exodus 15:1–2, 3–4, 5–6, 17–18 (1b)

FOURTH READING	Isaigh 54:5–14
Responsorial Psalm	Psalm 30:2, 4, 5–6, 11–12, 13 (2a)

FIFTH READING	Isaigh 55:1–11
Responsorial Psalm	Isaiah 12:2–3, 4, 5–6 (3)

SIXTH READING	Baruch 3:9–15, 32—4:4
Responsorial Psalm	Psalm 19:8, 9, 10, 11

A When baptism is celebrated, responsorial A is used
Isaiah 12:2–3, 4abcd, 5–6
B When baptism is not celebrated, responsorial B or C is used
Psalm 51:12–13, 14–15, 18–19
C When baptism is not celebrated: Epistle Romans 6:3–11
Psalm 118:1–2, 22–23

All is made to reveal God. We are made in God's own image. And we are liberated and brought out of bondage and slavery by the strong arm of God at the Red Sea as our God opens a way in the waters for us. And now God has opened a way in Jesus and in the waters of baptism. We are drawn into the waters, down in the tomb with Jesus and now we rise up, living no longer for ourselves alone, but hidden with Christ in God. Jesus bursts forth from the tomb, trailing light and glory into the world. Death is undone forever. It is life, and our God of compassion, of friendship and hope that has the last word. We live now, forever, in God. Our resurrections—the gift of Easter that will be given to all of us who believe—begins in our baptisms. We celebrate this day that our God has made and rejoice in our resurrection life. From here on, we practice resurrection for all creation to see and take heart from. Christ is risen. Alleluia.

Tonight we tell the story, from the beginning as all were made and it was so good. And we are the image of God, together. And we sing in between the readings for all the wonder and good-ness of God shared with us as God seeks to take us forward, ever more into the heart of life—through Abraham and Isaac—the only sacrifice, that of obedience. Then we are brought out (exodus) with the mighty arm of God into freedom and a land that must be in-ternal and shared, not just external geography. Then we hear the prophets through the ages calling us back, promising more life, deeper and truer, shared among all, especially the poor and those hungry and thirsty for life and justice. And lastly we are told we are made clean and whole in the waters of baptism, the blood of Christ crucified and risen from the dead, confirmed in justice and Spirit and made One in God together in Eucharist and Resurrection. It's the whole story, impossible to really tell. It must be lived again this year in God, with each other. Listen, sing, feel the water and oil, exalt and eat. We are set free. We are holy. We are one with Christ in God the Father, and the Spirit. Amen. Alleluia!

God creates by word of mouth and all is good, all is bound together in wholeness and beauty. And lastly we are made in the divine image to care for/have dominion over all that has been entrusted to us—as we are entrusted to God's care. And God rests, contemplates all and it is good. It is very very good.

Abraham is put to the test—asked to give up what is most precious and dear to him and to trust in God. When he obeys he is given back what was so important to him and a promise of hope, of generations to come after him. We are a part of those descendants who are to live in trust of God, and give to God what we treasure most—our own lives and those we love. (These are the first two readings of the night vigil. Together they are meant to be a narrative telling of the wonders that God has done for us reminding us that Jesus and the Resurrection comes at the end of a long history of compassion, being drawn to freedom, forgiven, shown mercy and made the beloved children of God—each and all of us.)

The women come to the tomb and hear the Easter message: a question! "Why do you look for the living among the dead? Remember all Jesus told you when he was with you! Remember his words about suffering and death and rising. "And they remember and run to tell the disciples, with trembling hearts of fear and hope. Others do not believe them—no surprises there! But Peter goes to the tomb and looks in and goes away wondering. We are told the same: Why do you look for the living among the dead. REMEMBER all that he told us when he was with us—the Word of the Scriptures. He is risen and he is alive!

SEASON OF EASTER

ABC   EASTER SUNDAY

FIRST READING   Acts 10:34a, 37–43
Responsorial Psalm   Psalm 118:1–2, 16–17, 22–23
SECOND READING   Colossians 3:1–4
                                            (or 1 Corinthians 5:6b–8)
GOSPEL   John 20:1–9

✴ It begins in the morning and Mary of Magdala and others go to the tomb, but the tomb is open and she runs to Peter and the other disciple that Jesus loved (never named because it is each of us, baptized) with the terrible announcement. The body of the Lord is gone. Peter and the other disciple run, Peter lagging behind. The other disciple waits for him to catch up and waits outside while Peter goes in, sees and does not understand. But the beloved disciple enters, sees and believes! The wonder and the power of the resurrection is beginning to be uncovered, the disciples stumbling towards understanding and the realization that he is alive and that death could not hold him bound—the Lord of life. We too, must begin by running to the empty tomb and seeing and hopefully believing. Lord, may we be your beloved disciples that wait on others and that see and believe because of love and faithfulness and your Word to us.

✴ Life begins to seep out into the world: in the words of Peter telling the story, testifying to the wisdom all who knew Jesus now know and must share. In the words of Paul crying out the glory of God in the risen Jesus and among all who live in the company of the Christ seated at God's right hand. We were dead. We are alive. Jesus was killed. Now he lives in glory—and with us—no more to die. His friends, Mary of Magdala, Peter and the one whom Jesus loved (all of us) go to the tomb and must enter (baptism) to be able to see and live in God. We must come to know and see and believe!

✲ This is Peter's sermon, a short succinct summary about Jesus who was killed, yet whom God has raised from the dead. The one who was 'hung on the tree' now lives and they have eaten with him. They have been commissioned to preach and bear witness to forgiveness and to the one set apart who is the judge of the living and the dead: the Son of Man, crucified and risen. We believe in Jesus. Our lives are now hidden with Christ in God. We are called to celebrate our new lives with the unleavened bread of sincerity and truth—God now is in the world, risen and in glory.

Mary comes to the tomb and runs to Simon Peter and the disciple whom Jesus loved and tells them that the body has been stolen and she and her companions don't know where it is. They run and the beloved disciple (never named for it is to be each of us) waits for Peter to enter the tomb. Love waits on authority even if it does not understand because the leader has sinned. And then Mary stays at the tomb weeping. She is looking for a body and cannot see Jesus who stands before her until he calls her by name—but he wants her to know him as the beloved Son of the Father, his Father and hers, the beloved Son of God, his God and hers. And this is what she must tell the disciples and learn that he is more than she ever thought he was—he is ascending to his Father and she cannot cling to her old perceptions of him. We too, must all let go of our small ideas of God and see the Crucified Risen God.

A   SECOND SUNDAY OF EASTER

FIRST READING   Acts 2:42–47
Responsorial Psalm   Psalm 118:2–4, 13–15, 22–24
SECOND READING   1 Peter 1:3–9
GOSPEL   John 20:19–31

✲ This is the culmination of the stories of Resurrection. Jesus enters the locked room and shows his crucified and risen body to the frightened disciples. He brings them the word that is Resurrection life: PEACE and breathes his own Spirit upon them, commanding them (and us) 'as the Father sent him, now he sends us' forth, out into the world to boldly give witness to forgiveness and mercy, yet also, with the power of the Spirit to call sin and evil what it is and to hold bound (and stop) those who do evil. This is what the power of the Spirit is given for in the world. Thomas isn't there (he doesn't believe them afterwards either) and he gives awful criteria for his personal belief. Jesus comes again after a week where they have tried in vain to share this news with Thomas. And Jesus holds Thomas bound—bound to his stopping the good news from getting out into the world, stopping hope and stopping the commission of the disciples because of his destructive and demeaning list of what will take him to personally believe. Jesus give them Peace again, of forgiveness, of truth-telling and of life. It is the Peace of the Father, the Peace of the Risen Lord and the Peace of the Spirit. It is Resurrection Peace and life.

B   SECOND SUNDAY OF EASTER

FIRST READING   Acts 4:32–35
Responsorial Psalm   Psalm 118:2–4, 13–15, 22–24
SECOND READING   1 John 5:1–6
GOSPEL   John 20:19–31

During this season we hear of the Body of Christ and what it looks like now—the community of believers holding all in common and its members doing for one another what they wanted to do for the crucified Body of Christ. And this day we hear the most powerful of the stories of Jesus Risen coming to his friends who are afraid, showing them the scars of his suffering and death, breathing upon them, giving over his own Spirit to them and sending them forth to do what he was sent by his Father into the world to do. But Thomas is missing and doesn't believe the community so Jesus must come again. It's a terrible piece of reality in the story of glory. We don't believe one another and so stop the Resurrection's power from getting out into the world and Jesus must come to show us how to confront one another with the truth. Do we look like the Risen Body of Christ?

C SECOND SUNDAY OF EASTER

FIRST READING   Acts 5:12–16
Responsorial Psalm   Psalm 118:2–4, 13–15, 22–24
SECOND READING   Revelation 1:9–11, 12–13, 17–19
GOSPEL   John 20:19–31

The church grows through the preaching and healings; and "many are added to the Lord," to the Body of Christ. The description of the peoples' needs echoes the descriptions of those who sought out Jesus' word and power. This is what we as Church should be attracting—by our preaching, call to conversion and care of the sick. John the beloved finds himself in exile for being a witness to Jesus and writes his love letters back to his community reminding them of the Son of Man who will come to judge the nations with justice—this Jesus is "the First and the Last and the One who lives." This is our God, Jesus, Crucified and Risen.

This is the Jesus who comes to his disciples who are in fear. And three times tells them, "Peace be with you," gives them his own Spirit and sends them out into the world to forgive and hold bound. This is the Jesus who admonishes Thomas for short-circuiting the gospel because of his own criteria and refusal to believe the others. This is Jesus that there is so much to say about that there aren't enough books that could be written about him. But we are given these stories—the essentials to build our faith upon.

A THIRD SUNDAY OF EASTER

FIRST READING   Acts 2:14, 22–33
Responsorial Psalm   Psalm 16:1–2, 5, 7–8, 9–10, 11
SECOND READING   1 Peter 1:17–21
GOSPEL   Luke 24:13–35

The story of the two disciples on the road to Emmaus, so familiar. But perhaps we need to look at the bulk of the story: Jesus' exegesis and preaching about himself—from the beginning with Moses, through all the prophets pointing out suffering as part of the whole history of those who speak the Word of God. For hours on the way he teaches them, stirring their hearts back to life with the Word of Scripture that is his presence among them, and among us as surely as the breaking of the bread. Peter in Acts stands up boldly in the power of the Spirit and preaches about this Jesus, a prophet mighty in word and deed but also risen from the dead by the power of the Spirit of God who is Crucified and Risen and who has given this Spirit to us to share with us. One of the primary ways to share this Spirit and life is to pour over the Scriptures together, stirring others' hearts back to life.

B   THIRD SUNDAY OF EASTER

FIRST READING   Acts 3:13–15, 17–19
Responsorial Psalm   Psalm 4:2, 4, 7–8, 9
SECOND READING   1 John 2:1–5a
GOSPEL   Luke 24:35–48

Peter continues to preach about God's servant Jesus, the Author of Life put to death and raised from the dead and we are his witnesses. And Peter calls out the words of Jesus: Reform your lives and be forgiven! This is the work of the Easter season for all of us: to know the Risen One among us, to remind one another as John does in his letters that if we know Jesus then we obey him and live in the truth, but if we do not keep his word, we are dead and do not know the love of God. It is in the Word of Scripture that we come to know and understand Jesus the Crucified and Risen One, in community. And in community we must live and suffer and be faithful, even unto death.

C   THIRD SUNDAY OF EASTER

FIRST READING   Acts 5:27–32, 40b–41
Responsorial Psalm   Psalm 30:2, 4, 5–6, 11–12, 13
SECOND READING   Revelation 5:11–14
GOSPEL   John 21:1–19

The church matures through persecution and resistance and rejoices in the struggle that brings others to hear the Name. And in heaven the Church and all creation rejoices in the presence, power and glory of the Lamb that was slain who receives praise and worship. This is John's vision but it is to be echoed on earth in small refrains and moments of worship.

The last story of John's gospel is the great catch—an image of the entire world that can be caught in the net of the Gospel, if the disciples obey Jesus' Word. And it is breakfast on the beach with Jesus serving his frightened, and insecure disciples. But all is forgiven and they are fed for the work of the coming of the kingdom of God upon the earth.

Peter walks with Jesus (reconciled) and three times professes his love. And he is given 3 penances to restore what he has rent with his betrayals: he is to tell the story of his sin and forgiveness (lambs); he is to forgive everyone everything as he has been forgiven (feed sheep); and he is to go out and search for the lost ones, as Jesus the Good Shepherd has found him (tend my sheep). This is the work of the church.

A   FOURTH SUNDAY OF EASTER

FIRST READING	Acts 2:1, 4a, 36–41
Responsorial Psalm	Psalm 23:1–3a, 3b–4, 5–6
SECOND READING	1 Peter 2:20b–25
GOSPEL	John 10:1–10

Reflection

✿ During the Easter season we listen to Acts and hear sermons, like Peter's today and how the early Church grew, nurtured on the Word of God and the Holy Spirit. Peter proclaims that God has made Jesus who they crucified Lord and Christ! And the people are deeply troubled, are converted and baptized, receiving the Spirit and saved from this crooked generation. Jesus preaches that he himself is the gate of the sheepfold that opens to let the sheep enter in and closes in protection and care. Jesus has come for one reason: that we might have life and life in all its fullness. Anyone else, everyone else is a robber and a thief. Do we hear the voice of the keeper of the sheep or do we listen to voices all around us? Do we belong to God alone or do we follow after others? Are we nurtured on the Word of God and the Spirit as the early Church matured?

B   FOURTH SUNDAY OF EASTER

FIRST READING   Acts 4:8–12
Responsorial Psalm   Psalm 118:1, 8–9, 21–23, 26, 28, 29
SECOND READING   1 John 3:1–2
GOSPEL   John 10:11–18

✻ The Easter power is the person, the presence of Jesus with us, in the Body of Christ, his own people. This name of Jesus (meaning one who saves the people) is the crucified and risen one among us now. One of the ways we image the Risen Christ among us is the Good Shepherd who protects the sheep with his very life. God in Jesus knows us, knows to whom we belong—God and one another— and we are called to listen only to Jesus' voice and follow him alone. We too are the beloved children of God with Jesus, called to lay down our lives with him for one another and even the sheep that aren't of the fold. Are we good sheep, beloved children and shepherds to one another?

C   FOURTH SUNDAY OF EASTER

FIRST READING   Acts 13:14, 43–52
Responsorial Psalm   Psalm 100:1–2, 3, 5
SECOND READING   Revelation 7:9, 14b–17
GOSPEL   John 10:27–30

✻ Now, Acts shifts into the telling of the story of Paul and Barnabas as they begin to travel and preach the Gospel. In Antioch they are rejected by the Jews and so they turn to the Gentiles who respond with delight and praise—and in response the persecution is initiated again. When they are expelled from the region they move on, filled with joy and the Spirit, shaking the dust from their feet (again echoes of Luke's gospel instruction on being sent out two by two to preach). And we hear/see the vision of John of all those who stayed faithful during the period of trial and been washed in the blood of the Lamb—they know shelter and feasting with the Lamb/Shepherd.

If we are Jesus' sheep then we hear only his voice and follow him. We know a taste of that joy, feasting, shelter now with the Good Shepherd, in fact we are in the hand of God. The Father and Jesus are one, and we dwell with them. We must do the work of God on earth and know the power/Spirit and share it with others.

A FIFTH SUNDAY OF EASTER

FIRST READING   Acts 6:1–7
Responsorial Psalm   Psalm 33:1–2, 4–5, 18–19
SECOND READING   1 Peter 2:4–9
GOSPEL   John 14:1–12

🌼 Trust in God and trust in me! We are not to be troubled, no matter what is going on in the world, in politics, among nations and in the church among one another. We are summoned to do the works of God, to continue the way, the truth and the life that Jesus has begun in the world. He is with us and yet he is also at God's hand preparing a way for us and he will come again to take us with him where he is. Jesus is our dwelling place and sanctuary in this world—he is now our life and way and our truth. He holds us together, binds us in love and sources all the good that we are to do, praying with us. Jesus is in the Father and Jesus is in us by our baptisms and birth in the Spirit. We are already one—but we must believe this amazing Good News and live in Jesus' name, drawing all together into the holiness of God.

B FIFTH SUNDAY OF EASTER

FIRST READING   Acts 9:26–31
Responsorial Psalm   Psalm 22:26–27, 28, 30, 31–32
SECOND READING   1 John 3:18–24
GOSPEL   John 15:1–8

🌼 Barnabas vouches for Saul even after the community remembers the harm and the violence he showed towards the earlier church. Barnabas is like Saul's godfather—sponsor who walks with him and leads him deeper into the heart of the community. And the church is at peace, growing stronger in the consolation of the Spirit. This is the historical description of John's letter: loving in deed and truth, at peace, no matter what happens, remaining in God, and God in us. And Jesus uses the image of the vine, the grower and the yield to express this vibrant life shared in the Word, eucharist and conversion. How is the vine today?

C   FIFTH SUNDAY OF EASTER

FIRST READING	Acts 14:21–27
Responsorial Psalm	Psalm 145:8–9, 10–11, 12–13
SECOND READING	Revelation 21:1–5a
GOSPEL	John 13:31–33a, 34–35

Paul and Barnabas return to bring reassurance and encouragement to the new churches, warning them of the reality of trials to come. They pray and fast and commend those chosen to be elders. They travel and tell of the good news spreading and the wide open door to the Gentiles. Again we hear/see the vision of John: how the work of Jesus and the work of the Spirit in the Church will one day come to fulfillment—there will be a new heaven and earth, a new Jerusalem come from heaven where God dwells with his people and there will be no suffering, weeping, mourning or pain—all things will be made new. This is what is happening now in the world by the work and the Word of God in the power of the Spirit.

Jesus the night before he dies, tells us, encouraging and reassuring that he will be raised up and glorified (crucified and risen from the dead) and even though he will not be with us (in the flesh) he wants to give us a new commandment: love one another. Such as my love has been for you, so must your love be for each other. This is how all will know you for my disciples: your love for one another. This is the new thing that will set in motion the new heavens and earth. It is up to us now to love like Jesus and to encourage one another and to choose new elders as the Church grows and spreads forth.

A   SIXTH SUNDAY OF EASTER

FIRST READING	Acts 8:5–8, 14–17
Responsorial Psalm	Psalm 66:1–3, 4–5, 6–7, 16, 20
SECOND READING	1 Peter 3:15–18
GOSPEL	John 14:15–21

✴ In this Easter season we are being taught by the Word of Jesus, the Scriptures, in the power of the Spirit all that is necessary for us to live and to love as the servants and friends of God in the world. Jesus speaks to us as intimates, those devoted to him and in love with God the Father as he has loved God the Father. We are invited into that love and by the power of the resurrection life shared with us in baptism we are all summoned to love, to express that love and live it out in the world, loving in obedience and gratefulness for having been so loved by God in Jesus. It is the gift of the Spirit, the first gift given to those who believe that it teaches us, reminds us, inheres in us, binding us as one to the Father and Jesus. We know that Jesus and we are one in the Father by the power of the Spirit who is our Helper. This Spirit is given in baptism, but it is given to the Church, to communities for help in loving in a world that resists and is not always open to the Word of God. We must remember and let the Spirit lay claim to our lives.

B   SIXTH SUNDAY OF EASTER

FIRST READING   Acts 10:25–26, 34–35, 44–48
Responsorial Psalm   Psalm 98:1, 2–3, 3–4
SECOND READING   1 John 4:7–10
GOSPEL   John 15:9–17

✴ Peter enters Cornelius' house and as he preaches the Spirit comes upon Cornelius and everyone there listening. They are baptized in the Spirit first, followed by water! It seems order of ritual wasn't that crucial. The power of the Word transforms. It is this Word that gives knowledge of God, and that knowledge is— its heart—Love. Love is the person Jesus revealed and dwelling in our midst, in word, eucharist, community, the poor. We are called friends of God IF we obey the commands of Jesus, even to loving unto death, as he did with us. And our God shares the joy of the Trinity with us, but we must remember that we have been chosen and that we are to bear fruit in the world. Always it comes down to: love one another as I have loved you.

C   SIXTH SUNDAY OF EASTER

FIRST READING   Acts 15:1–2, 22–29
Responsorial Psalm   Psalm 67:2–3, 5, 6, 8
SECOND READING   Rev 21:10–14, 22–23
GOSPEL   John 14:23–29

✺ The Church needs to hear often that we are to lay no burden on believers beyond what is strictly necessary and that the Holy Spirit decides what is needed—based on the words of Jesus. Those who cause dissension by demanding their own agenda must be pointed out as those who cause disturbance and those who preach the gospel must be acknowledged as those belonging to and are under the power of the Lord and the Spirit. Again, when we get bogged down in details and laws/customs/traditions we tend to forget the vision of what we have been given to share and to live— that there is no temple in the city. The Lord, God, the Almighty is its temple and he and the Lamb are its light and life.

Our God is the Trinity and if we are true to the Word of Jesus then God the Father comes and dwells within us. And if we take this Word to heart the Spirit, the Paraclete will be sent to us in the name of Jesus to instruct us, remind us, and teach us—but most especially to bring us the peace of Christ that is Jesus' gift to us. This peace is given so that we are not distressed or fearful, or racked with dissenters but that we live as one in God, the Trinity.

A   THE ASCENSION OF THE LORD

FIRST READING   Acts 1:1–11
Responsorial Psalm   Psalm 47:2–3, 6–7, 8–9
SECOND READING   Ephesians 1:17–23
GOSPEL   Matthew 28:16–20

Jesus departs from the earth, drawing his disciples to the mountain where he commissions them to go out into the whole world, make disciples, baptize in the name of the Father, the Son and the Spirit (the first time the Trinity is clearly mentioned in the gospel) and to teach all that he has commanded us to do. We are to make disciples by example and to pray and become one in the Trinity. The community was sent to wait, as he left them, to send them the gift of the Spirit that would bind them together in him, teaching them and preparing them to go boldly into the world, as the Father had sent him into the world, to us. They are found waiting together, praying for the power that will come from on high, come from God. They are waiting to be baptized in the Holy Spirit. We wait, again as church, as communities and believers for the Spirit to be given once again so that the power of God may move out into the world again, in us.

B   THE ASCENSION OF THE LORD

FIRST READING   Acts 1:1–11
Responsorial Psalm   Psalm 47:2–3, 6–7, 8–9
SECOND READING   Ephesians 4:1–13
                                   (or Ephesians 4:1–7, 11–13)
GOSPEL   Mark 16:15–20

We return to the beginning of Acts to celebrate the Ascension, of the crucified and risen Jesus instructing the believers to wait and receive the Spirit together as he disappears from their sight (he does not leave us). It is time to wait together to be baptized with the Spirit, not as individuals but as the Body of Christ in the world. We are told that we are witnesses and other questions we might have will not be answered. We are to stick to the core—the heart of the Word of God. This is wisdom, to know Jesus and the power of God in Jesus. The whole world is waiting for this wisdom but we must wait for the Spirit to fill us with God's power and word.

C   THE ASCENSION OF THE LORD

FIRST READING   Acts 1:1–11
Responsorial Psalm   Psalm 47:2–3, 6–7, 8–9
SECOND READING   Hebrews 9:24–28; 10:19–23
GOSPEL   Luke 24:46–53

Luke writes to Theophilus that he wrote about Jesus' works, words, life and death, and resurrection and the power of the Spirit of God at work in Jesus. And now he writes about the work of the power of the Spirit of God in the church, those who believe in Jesus, as proof that Jesus is risen and still with us. Jesus sent the disciples into the city to wait for the promise and the power of the Spirit that will make them witnesses to the ends of the earth. And Jesus is lifted up before them and disappears. The angels proclaim that 'this Jesus taken up into heaven will one day return'. The Ascension is the departure of Jesus, the Word made flesh, from the earth so that the Spirit of Jesus, the Risen Lord may be sent to those who believe.

All that is taught and written, prayed and ritualized is begun in the name of the Father, the Son and the Spirit. This Spirit will bring us wisdom, enlightenment, hope, and the heritage that is ours by baptism and confirmation—and we will know the immeasurable scope of the power of God if we believe. We are clothed with this power in baptism and confirmation and we are clothed with this power as Church on Pentecost and when we gather as Church to worship God.

A SEVENTH SUNDAY OF EASTER

FIRST READING   Acts 1:12–14
Responsorial Psalm   Psalm 27:1, 4, 7–8
SECOND READING   1 Peter 4:13–16
GOSPEL   John 17:1–11

Now Jesus prays to the Father asking for God to give him glory so that he might give glory to God. He has worked and glorified God in his words, his works, his disciples, his prayer—in everything. He has given away everything that the Father has given to him and they received it, as best as they could and so Jesus prays for them, his disciples and for all of us because we will need it. He prays that we will stay in God, that we will be kept in his Name and that we will be one as Jesus and the Father are one. We could spend years pouring over this prayer, seeking to learn what Jesus knows of God and how he loves him, glorifies him and serves him, knowing that he is rejected, misunderstood even by those who want to follow him and that he will be crucified—and glorified in dying with trust and love for God and forgiveness of those who kill him. It is close to the time of leaving us and we need Jesus' prayers. Jesus' prayers are with us always now and we know them in the gift of the Spirit.

B SEVENTH SUNDAY OF EASTER

FIRST READING — Acts 1:15–17
Responsorial Psalm — Psalm 103:1–2, 11–12, 19–20
SECOND READING — 1 John 4:11–16
GOSPEL — John 17:11b–19

✴ Jesus continues praying for us so that we will be kept in God's Name, in communion of heart and life. While he was with us in the flesh he held us together in his presence but now he is coming home to the Father and he leaves us with his words that will bring joy to us. His word is his gift to us, for protection, for courage, insight, understanding, power and truth and we are to hold fast to this Word and stay in the world and know that Jesus has prayed that we will be kept from the evil one that hinders us from living as the children of God. Jesus consecrates us in truth, in God's word and his own word to us. And we will be sent into the world, as Jesus was, consecrated in Jesus' word, and in his body given as sacrifice in death. This is the only sacrifice that God wants of us—what Jesus gave—his word, his life and his obedience in love. This is what Jesus prays that we give to God.

C SEVENTH SUNDAY OF EASTER

FIRST READING — Acts 7:55–60
Responsorial Psalm — Psalm 97:1–2, 6–7, 9
SECOND READING — Revelation 22:12–14, 16–17, 20
GOSPEL — John 17:20–26

✴ Paul is released from prison and he is brought before the Sanhedrin to be tried. Paul is shrewd and says that he is a Pharisee and that he stands before them because he believes in the resurrection (setting the factions against each other). A riot breaks out and he is rescued by the troops and taken back to headquarters. Paul dreams that the Lord is at his side and he is told to have courage. He has testified to Jesus in Jerusalem, now he will testify to the risen Lord in Rome. Paul does have a way of enraging people—perhaps we need to learn more from Jesus' ways and words, than from Paul's style and weaknesses on how to preach the good news of the crucified and risen Lord.

Jesus prays for all who believe, for all who teach/preach and prays that we all might be one as the Father is one in him and he is in the Father and that all of us might be one in God, as they are in communion. We are given to know the Father, to know the Word made flesh, and Jesus will continue to reveal God to us in the Spirit. Does this love and life of God dwell in us? How do we as church reveal this to the world today?

A   PENTECOST SUNDAY

FIRST READING   Acts 2:1–11
Responsorial Psalm   Psalm 104:1, 24, 29–30, 31, 34
SECOND READING   1 Corinthians 12:3b–7, 12–13
GOSPEL   John 20:19–23

We read again the Easter appearance of the Risen Lord to his disciples in the upper room, bringing them the Peace of Resurrection, the power over suffering and death, his showing forth of his wounds in his body and the gift of the Spirit breathed upon them, sending them forth into the world, as the Father sent him. The power of the Spirit is given to forgive and to hold bound the world when it comes to sin, evil and injustice. There is no place on earth where our God can be kept out and resurrection life seeps into every corner of the world. Now we are to be witnesses to the power of the Cross, the Truth of Jesus' words and the proclamation of forgiveness and hope—we are one with God and meant to live in communion and peace. Peace be with you. Peace be with us all. Peace be to the world.

B   PENTECOST SUNDAY

FIRST READING   Acts 2:1–11
Responsorial Psalm   Psalm 104:1, 24, 29–30, 31, 34
SECOND READING   Galatians 5:16–25
GOSPEL   John 15:26–27; 16:12–15

The fifty days of rejoicing in the Risen Lord have been completed and now we are to be clothed from on high with the gift of the Father, sent at the bequest of Jesus: the Spirit. The

Spirit comes for boldness, courage, proclamation, witness, public commitment, diversity and communion, unity and freedom for all the children of God. The Spirit was meant to be let loose and shared aloud publicly not hoarded individually, or even contained in small groups. All Easter we have listened to how the Word/Spirit spread through the world, unstoppable. The Body of Christ is one, but belongs to all the earth. Receive the Spirit and Go!

C   PENTECOST SUNDAY

FIRST READING   Acts 2:1–11
Responsorial Psalm   Psalm 104:1, 24, 29–30, 31, 34
SECOND READING   Romans 8:8–17
GOSPEL   John 14:15–16, 23b–26

The Spirit comes upon all those gathered and waiting to be clothed with power from on high and all begin to express the Spirit in foreign tongues, preaching boldly. Everyone who hears them, understands in their own language what God has done in Jesus. This Spirit has been given to us, individually in confirmation but more powerfully as Church together. We gather and the Spirit is expressed in each/all of us. We all call God "Father," in the power of the Spirit and we are all gifted, These gifts are for the communion of the Church, and the common good. We are all one in the Spirit by baptism and eucharist.

The Spirit is Peace, the Person of the Risen Lord breathed into us, poured out upon us, sending us out into the world, as the Father sent Jesus to preach forgiveness and to hold those who do evil/injustice/violence bound—to resist evil and to live under the power of the sign of the cross. The Spirit draws us into the Trinity with Jesus to the glory of the Father. We can spend the rest of our lives/prayers seeking to understand this mystery.

ORDINARY TIME

A SECOND SUNDAY IN ORDINARY TIME

FIRST READING — Isaiah 49:3:5–6
Responsorial Psalm — Psalm 40:2–4, 7–8, 8–9, 10
SECOND READING — 1 Corinthians 1:1–3
GOSPEL — John 1:29–34

✻ Who is Jesus? This is the question at the root of all the readings these weeks after Epiphany and now, into Ordinary Time. Now we are told: he is the Lamb of God! The image of Exodus when the blood of the sacrificed lamb was smeared on the doorposts of the Israelites to defend them from death. This is the one John the Baptizer has waited and prepared way for—and now he is here. And John declares emphatically that this is the Chosen One of God whom he baptized but really had no idea who He truly was standing before.

Who is Jesus? Do we see the fullness of God residing in Jesus, the Prophet of God, the Word of God made flesh among us, the pity and compassion of God touching and reaching out to us while calling us to the truth, to repent and to change in every area of our thoughts, ways and relationships? What Jesus are we witnesses to in our time?

B SECOND SUNDAY IN ORDINARY TIME

FIRST READING — 1 Samuel 3:3b–10, 19
Responsorial Psalm — Psalm 40:2, 4, 7–8, 8–9, 10
SECOND READING — 1 Corinthians 6:13c–15a, 17–20
GOSPEL — John 1:35–42

✻ Today John sees and recognizes Jesus, points him out and calls him the Lamb of God. He witnesses that this is the One the Spirit came upon, and so he will baptize with the Spirit of God. His witness is profound: "I have seen! And I declare that is the Chosen One of God." John witnesses in words as a prophet. We too are prophets, but by our baptisms we are to proclaim the presence of Jesus among us in our lives and works. Do we know this Lamb of God, who is always with those in need, those shunned and those who are the victims of the world's violence? Do we see the Lamb of God among us?

C SECOND SUNDAY IN ORDINARY TIME

FIRST READING   Isaiah 62:1–5
Responsorial Psalm   Psalm 96:1–2, 2–3, 7–8, 9–10
SECOND READING   1 Corinthians 12:4–11
GOSPEL   John 2:1–11

The messiah is a bridegroom, and the people of God are God's 'delight.' God rejoices in us, bringing us vindication, glory and hope in the presence of our God. We live at the wedding feast (Baptism, Confirmation and Eucharist) and have been overwhelmed with gifts: the manifestation of the Spirit for the common good—a feast for the people so that all our needs are taken care of. This is the wedding feast—the church, the Body of Christ, the people of God and there is always more than enough for everyone, even after the celebration of the presence of God among us. It is only the servants in the back room who know where the wine came from (waters/baptism) into the wine of Eucharist and the feast, the kingdom of God only comes through obedience: "do whatever he tells us"—echoes of the Father's words: listen to him, obey! Can we be found among the disciples of Jesus? Are we unaware of the mysteries of our faith or are we the servants who obey?

A THIRD SUNDAY IN ORDINARY TIME

FIRST READING   Isaiah 8:23—9:3
Responsorial Psalm   Psalm 27:1, 4, 13–14
SECOND READING   1 Corinthians 1:10–13, 17
GOSPEL   Matthew 4:12–23

Again we hear the wrap up of what Jesus is trying to do—what he has been sent into the world to do: to preach, fulfill the words of the prophets, bring light to those in darkness and fear; preach conversion and open peoples' eyes to the kingdom that has come in his own presence and body among us. And he calls disciples to his side so that they follow along with him, learning by watching, hearing and being in his presence, associated with him.

Again we are summoned and asked if our lives reflect what Jesus is intent on doing in the world? Are we preaching hope, justice and life for the poorest, the hungry of the earth (more than 80% of the world) and a call to change the way we live, what we do with our resources and income, our excess and our privilege and power in the world? Have we left the ways of the world: profit, greed, insensitivity to the pain of the majority, self-absorption, acceptability and the values of our nation to choose instead the company of Jesus and breaking the Word and the bread with him?

B   THIRD SUNDAY IN ORDINARY TIME

FIRST READING   Jonah 3:1–5, 10
Responsorial Psalm   Psalm 25:4–5, 6–7, 8–9
SECOND READING   1 Corinthians 7:29–31
GOSPEL   Mark 1:14–20

Jonah goes forth into the city of Nineveh and calls them to repentance. His cry is a warning and an announcement and amazingly the whole city repents, fasts and desists from their evil ways. And God in turn repents and does not do justice to them. Paul warns us that time is short and we should be repenting too— turning from evil and concentrating on living in the world of the Word made flesh. John is arrested and Jesus begins to cry out "This is the time! Today! The reign of God is at hand—reach out and touch it in another human being! Reform your lives and believe, live the good news! And he summons those who will be his own on the spot. Today we are summoned again. Now, forget about putting things in order. Abandon what is unnecessary and go off in his company. It's time.

C THIRD SUNDAY IN ORDINARY TIME

FIRST READING   Nehemiah 8:2–4a, 5–6, 8–10
Responsorial Psalm   Psalm 19:8, 9, 10, 15
SECOND READING   1 Corinthians 12:12–30
GOSPEL   Luke 1:1–4; 4:14–21

✺ The book of the law is read to the whole assembly from daybreak to midday! They listened attentively with their eyes on the scroll. They weep for the words and Ezra interpreted them to the people. And they are encouraged to the feast of rich foods and sweet drinks , allotting portions to those who had nothing—for the day is holy to the Lord. This is the description of church! We are the body of Christ, all members of the same flesh, heart, mind and spirit in the Lord. All are needed and are bound as one. All suffer, all rejoice as one, and all serve the others. All are one though there are many—diverse nations, races, children, men/women.

The Gospel of Luke begins with the writing to Theophilius for his instruction, and to help him remember what he was originally taught. And it is Jesus, in the power of the Spirit and the Word made flesh that teaches us all. He stands in the synagogue at Nazareth and reads from the scroll of the prophet Isaiah. This is the work of God in Jesus: good news to the poor, liberty to captives, new sight to the blind, free the oppressed and announce this year as mercy from the Lord. It begins here, in us, the Body of Christ, when we hear, we believe and we obey.

A FOURTH SUNDAY IN ORDINARY TIME

FIRST READING   Zephaniah 2:3, 3:12–13
Responsorial Psalm   Psalm 146:6–7, 8–9, 9–10
SECOND READING   1 Corinthians 1:26–31
GOSPEL   Matthew 5:1–12a

✺ This is the sermon on the mountain, the eight blessings of what it means to believe in Jesus, to dwell in the kingdom of justice and peace here and now and what we will both experience here on earth and know later in fullness. Eight groups of people are blessed now: the poor, the mourners, the gentle (non-violent); those who hunger and thirst for justice; the merciful, the pure in heart, those who work for peace and those persecuted like the prophets who called for justice for the poor as the way to honor and obey God alone. This is Jesus' call to rejoice if we find ourselves in these groups because of our words, our associations with other people, our choices and works for justice and mercy. The first and the last are in the present tense—to find ourselves among the poor and persecuted for justice puts us in the kingdom with Jesus now. The others will know more of it as it comes to fruition in the world. Each saying is a parable in itself—seeking to startle and catch us off guard. Do we dwell in the kingdom now? Who do we need to associate ourselves with now, befriend them and dwell close to them to know this blessing here on earth now?

B FOURTH SUNDAY IN ORDINARY TIME

FIRST READING   Deuteronomy 18:15–20
Responsorial Psalm   Psalm 95:1–2, 6–7, 7–9
SECOND READING   1 Corinthians 7:32–35
GOSPEL   Mark 1:21–28

Moses declares to the people that there will come a prophet like him that God will raise up among them and they are to listen to him. And this prophet will speak only in the name of God, and God himself will hold him accountable for his words. We are told to obey this prophet. And Jesus enters the synagogue on the Sabbath and teaches with authority and power, like Moses! And someone who is mentally ill, distraught in mind and body cries out "What do you want of us, Jesus of Nazareth?" You who are the Holy One of God! He is muted and given his own self/mind back by the Word of God. It seems those who recognize who Jesus is might be those among us who are the most twisted in mind and helpless to control themselves. But Jesus has power over all things, all peoples and all that is good and evil among us. Do we want to be seen and told "Be quiet! Come out of them!" by Jesus?

C   FOURTH SUNDAY IN ORDINARY TIME

FIRST READING	Jeremiah 1:4–5, 17–19
Responsorial Psalm	Psalm 71:1–2, 3–4, 5–6, 15–17
SECOND READING	1 Corinthians 12:31—13:13
GOSPEL	Luke 4:21–30

This is the calling of the prophet—from before he was born in his mother's womb. He is known, dedicated and charged with the Word and no matter what happens, God is with him to deliver him. And we too have been called, dedicated and charged, and given the Word and gifts besides, specifically the gift or the calling to live with love: love that is down to earth, practical, careful of the needy, treating them with the love God has shown to us all, a love that is patient, sensitive to others, holding others in high regard, rejoicing with others. Love never fails. How are we at loving—one another, family, neighbors, the Body of Christ/church and our nation and enemies?

Jesus is a prophet and those in his own family, his neighborhood and even religious community refused to listen to him—they kept him in categories where they could see him as they wanted him to be, and so not listen to him. First they are amazed and then they are skeptical and then they seek to kill him, filled with indignation and self-righteousness. Are we prophets, followers of the Word of the Lord? Are we supportive of prophets in our times/places or are we indignant at being told the truth and so react in violence?

A   FIFTH SUNDAY IN ORDINARY TIME

FIRST READING	Isaiah 58:7–10
Responsorial Psalm	Psalm 112:4–5, 6–7, 8–9
SECOND READING	1 Corinthians 2:1–5
GOSPEL	Matthew 5:13–16

We are told what we are—salt of the earth, light for the world, those who show forth the Father's goodness to others so that they come to praise our Father. How? Isaiah reminds us: Share our bread with the hungry, provide shelter and dignity, care for our own—be compassionate, enlarge the boundaries of our justice and care for others and our light will break forth like the dawn! And in so doing we will be healed, our prayers heard and God will be near us. But we must be on guard not to lose our saltiness—not to resist or take the Word of God for granted or to let our light go out—or lost in the world's false brightness, as the stars cannot be seen because of the lights of a city dimming their sight. We, together, and separately must practice justice and be holy if we are the beloved children of our Father.

B FIFTH SUNDAY IN ORDINARY TIME

FIRST READING   Job 7:1–4, 6–7
Responsorial Psalm   Psalm 147:1–2, 3–4, 5–6
SECOND READING   1 Corinthians 9:16–19, 22–23
GOSPEL   Mark 1:29–39

We hear what life is like from Job's point of view: misery, drudgery, like the wind, seemingly filled with resentment and longing. Paul tells his churches that they are entrusted with the good news, sharing its blessings in gratitude, and are to be the slaves of all, with a view to winning the weak. And Jesus lives fully, praying with others in the synagogue, going home with friends, to heal and be waited upon. Then as word spreads, he attends to the needs of the crowds, and then disappears to be with his Father alone all night until his disciples come looking for him. He rises and goes forth to proclaim the Gospel and undoing evil, setting the children of God free to live in grace. This is life in God.

C FIFTH SUNDAY IN ORDINARY TIME

FIRST READING   Isaiah 6:1–2a, 3–8
Responsorial Psalm   Psalm 138:1–2, 2–3, 4–5, 7–8
SECOND READING   1 Corinthians 15:1–11
GOSPEL   Luke 5:1–11

Isaiah meets the Holy One in the temple and knows his own sinfulness. Yet he is seared with coals and his mouth is purged of wickedness. And in response to God's cry: "Whom shall I send? Who will go for us?" he responds boldly: "Here I am, send me". And Isaiah goes forth. Paul reminds us that he has gone forth to preach the gospel that is saving us even now and that he hands on to us what he received. By God's favor, we are all what we are—what we are called to be by God to preach, each in our own time.

Jesus teaches by the lake and then goes into one of the boats moored there (Peter's) and orders him to cast out—out in the deep and let down nets for a catch. They had fished all night and caught nothing (they fished trawling along the shore, afraid of the deep—they could not swim). Simon is afraid, but he obeys and they make a great catch. The first to be caught is Peter, falling on his knees knowing he too is not worthy to be in the presence of Jesus. But all of them, and us are told "Do not be afraid, for now on you will be catching men and women." They left it all and became his followers. We too have been called. How are we doing with the catch? Have we left everything and become followers? Who do we preach to, with?

B   SIXTH SUNDAY IN ORDINARY TIME

FIRST READING   Leviticus 13:1–2, 44–46
Responsorial Psalm   Psalm 32:1–2, 5, 11
SECOND READING   1 Corinthians 10:31—11:1
GOSPEL   Mark 1:40–45

The law of Moses in regard to lepers sought to protect the people from a disease that they thought was contagious. The lepers were to avoid the people. They were outcast and live on the fringe of the people. Only the priest could declare the leper clean again. Jesus wills the cure of the leper who comes to him and reaches out to touch him, disobeying the law that doubly inflicts pain on the one who was sick. He is cautioned to be quiet but he tells everyone what Jesus had done for him, in the process pushing Jesus outside the community as bearing the danger of contagion in himself now. Yet people come to him. And we are commanded to imitate Christ, to touch the outcast and the sick and to will the life of all excluded from society by old laws and traditions based on ignorance and fear. Do we imitate Christ?

C   SIXTH SUNDAY IN ORDINARY TIME

FIRST READING   Jeremiah 17:5–8
Responsorial Psalm   Psalm 1:1–2, 3, 4–6
SECOND READING   1 Corinthians 15:12, 16–20
GOSPEL   Luke 6:17, 20–26

We are called to choose which we will be: the one who stands in a waste, trusting the world and its peoples, or the one who trusts in God and is planted along running waters and bearing fruit in every season. Choose! We choose Christ risen from the dead because by baptism we now know the fruits of resurrection. And Jesus teaches us how to live the life of resurrection in the four blessings and the four woes, reminding us that it is the poor, those who hunger and weep and those who are persecuted for the gospel who know the Kingdom and the presence of God so strongly and that those who play the world and are rich, satisfied, foolish, those who persecute others for the gospel, listening only to false prophets who tell them what they want to hear, are far from God and the kingdom—standing in the waste. Choose! And we must choose together.

B   SEVENTH SUNDAY IN ORDINARY TIME

FIRST READING   Isaiah 43:18–19, 21–22, 24b–25
Responsorial Psalm   Psalm 41:2–3, 4–5, 13–14
SECOND READING   2 Corinthians 1:18–22
GOSPEL   Mark 2:1–12

We are witnesses to the new things that God is doing, making a people for himself, making a desert into a land of springs and life, and he is forgiving us, wiping out our sins and transgressions. God is faithful and keeps his word. And in our baptisms, sealed in the Spirit, we are to learn to be "Yes ," always "Yes" as the sons and daughters of God. Jesus heals a man brought to him by his friends, lowered through the roof, and he heals him because of his friends' belief. We are summoned to be friends like that to one another, bringing one another in our weakness and sin before God, doing new things with God in the world. There is no limit to the power of God in us, if we are "yes" and we seek to share the Spirit that has been given to us.

C   SEVENTH SUNDAY IN ORDINARY TIME

FIRST READING   1 Samuel 26:2, 7–9, 12–13, 22–23
Responsorial Psalm   Psalm 103:1–2, 3–4, 8, 10, 12–13
SECOND READING   1 Corinthians 15:45–49
GOSPEL   Luke 6:27–38

Saul goes hunting David—one man against an army of 3000! It is David who finds Saul by night and takes his spear and water jug, and does not kill him. The Lord rewards justice and faithfulness, not killing and murder—David's greatness is that he did not kill when he could have! We are called as people who live upon the earth but we bear the likeness of God and so we must act as God acts.

And so Jesus tells us what that is like: love our enemies (it is repeated again and again) and do good to all, even those who harm us or those we fear. We are to react to violence and aggression with human restraint and imagination. We are to give generously to all, lending to others in need. We are to be compassionate like God (like God has always been to us!) and we re to forgive and pardon. This is to be our greatness if we bear the likeness of God upon us.

B   EIGHTH SUNDAY IN ORDINARY TIME

FIRST READING   Hosea 2:16–17, 21–22
Responsorial Psalm   Psalm 103:1–2, 3–4, 8, 10, 12–13
SECOND READING   2 Corinthians 3:1–6
GOSPEL   Mark 2:18–22

God is always seeking us out to draw us back to Him, to lead us and speak to our hearts. But we wander and do not respond. And still God wants to be intimate with us, bound to us in love and mercy, in justice forever, so that we will know God. This is our true nature.

Paul reminds us that we are God's love letters written in the Spirit for all to read. And Jesus tries in vain to tell us that we are the guests at a wedding feast with God. We are to live rejoicing, feasting on this intimacy with God. There will come a day when we must fast and we lose the presence of Jesus, but until that day comes, there is a freshness and a life in the world that is new and holy.

We have this presence. Listen, eat, drink and rejoice.

A TENTH SUNDAY IN ORDINARY TIME

FIRST READING	Hosea 6:3–6
Responsorial Psalm	Psalm 50:1, 8, 12–13, 14–15
SECOND READING	Romans 4:18–25
GOSPEL	Matthew 9:9–13

Jesus calls a disciple—this one, Matthew, a minor tax collector who would have been despised by his neighbors for being in collusion with Rome, their oppressors and making a living off the taxation and injustice that they were subject to. Matthew not only follows him, but throws a party for his friends, to meet Jesus and Jesus goes! And he is criticized. Jesus is blunt with the good religious, self-righteous ones: Read the Scriptures about what God wants: "What I want is mercy, not sacrifice. I did not come to call the righteous but sinners." He is mocking them—they have reduced the desire of God down to empty ritual and organized religion, rather than its heart and soul—conversion and holiness and forgiveness of others that lures them back into community and the practice of forgiveness and justice in gratitude. Jesus is calling us. Which group would he find us in—the religious self-righteous or those knowing they have been touched by mercy?

A ELEVENTH SUNDAY IN ORDINARY TIME

FIRST READING	Exodus 19:2–6a
Responsorial Psalm	Psalm 100:1–2, 3, 5
SECOND READING	Romans 5:6–11
GOSPEL	Matthew 9:36—10:8

✤ Always there are crowds of people pressing in around Jesus and so many in such desperate need moves Jesus to great pity and compassion, but also to exhort his disciples to pray for more workers—twelve is nothing—there should be one thousand two hundred in every church to gather the harvest that others have sown and that the Spirit brings to readiness. Jesus picks his disciples, twelve in remembrance of the twelve tribes of Israel, but there are supposed to be disciples from every tribe, race, nation, place and peoples on earth. And these leaders are given authority over unclean spirits—to stand and confront evil, sin and injustice that harms and hinders the children of God and to heal every disease and sickness—to provide solace, medicine, comfort, balm, peace and forgiveness for every malady that exists. These are the primary functions of the apostles. And in every group there are those with great weakness: Peter, Thomas, James and John the sons of Thunder and all will fight among themselves for power and there are those who will betray all that the group seeks to witness to—we must be aware of our own weakness and sins and that they effect the coming of the kingdom among us.

C ELEVENTH SUNDAY IN ORDINARY TIME

FIRST READING   2 Samuel 12:7–10, 13
Responsorial Psalm   Psalm 32:1–2, 5, 7, 11
SECOND READING   Galatians 2:16, 19–21
GOSPEL   Luke 7:36—8:3

✤ Nathan attacks David with the truth of his sin, despite after all the goodness God has done for him. He has murdered to marry another man's wife. David has despised God. David acknowledges his sin, is forgiven and will not die. We all have sinned and despised God, on our own, in collusion with others, our government and others but do we acknowledge our sin? In baptism we heard these words: "I have been crucified with Christ, and the life I live now is not my own; Christ is living in me." Have we made that precious gift pointless, like David and so many others? Or, as in the gospel, do we follow in gratitude like the women who seek to care for Jesus as he has cared for them?

This is the story of a Pharisee who invites Jesus to dinner. A woman comes and anoints Jesus' feet, weeping and drying them with her hair. She scandalizes the host who has not treated Jesus with respect. He disdains the woman and Jesus, so Jesus tells him a parable about forgiveness of debts/sins. Who loves him more—the one who is forgiven little, or the one who is forgiven much? She is forgiven much because of her love and yet the Pharisee doesn't even know that he is in even greater need that she is—because of his lack of hospitality, his disdain and lack of respect for either of them, his judgment and self-righteousness. And what of us—how much do we need to be forgiven?

A   TWELFTH SUNDAY IN ORDINARY TIME

FIRST READING	Jeremiah 20:10–13
Responsorial Psalm	Psalm 69:8–10, 14, 17, 33–35
SECOND READING	Romans 5:12–15
GOSPEL	Matthew 10:26–33

There will be hard times, but there will be justice and all will be uncovered. We have been taught by Light and we must shout what we have heard in the Gospel from the house tops no matter what is happening in the world. We must stand and resist with words of truth and not be afraid of what those with power in the world can do to us—and they can do some terrible things: physically, to those we love, to our hopes and dreams, our securities, our daily lives and jobs, our persons. God remembers us and holds us in his mind and hand and we are precious to our God, especially when we are suffering in any way because we are bound to God. We must live with the courage of the Spirit and the gifts of our baptism and confirmation, with grace to endure and stand up with Jesus truthfully, without harm and for those who are hurt. This is our resurrection life that began in baptism and we practice this all our lives, in good times and hard times, alone if need be, and with our communities.

B TWELFTH SUNDAY IN ORDINARY TIME

FIRST READING   Job 38:1, 8–11
Responsorial Psalm   Psalm 107:23–24, 25–26, 28–29, 30–31
SECOND READING   2 Corinthians 5:14–17
GOSPEL   Mark 4:35–41

God is the Lord/maker of creation and his power is revealed in the skies/clouds, and the waters of the sea, in limitless wonder and in bounds set by God's design. This is our God revealed in Jesus as Father. We are baptized into God, and live no longer for ourselves alone, but hidden with Christ in God. Our lives have meaning in a much larger design than anything we can know. Jesus too is Lord of heaven and earth, the beloved son of the Father, working in the Spirit. How strong is our faith? How consistent? How much do we really know the person of Jesus Christ, Lord?

A THIRTEENTH SUNDAY IN ORDINARY TIME

FIRST READING   2 Kings 4:8–11, 14–16a
Responsorial Psalm   Psalm 89:2–3, 16–17, 18–19
SECOND READING   Romans 6:3–4, 8–11
GOSPEL   Matthew 10:37–42

Who do we love? And who do we love best? Seems a strange question but Jesus is clear that we must love God and one another more than we love our parents, children, husband and wife, family. We are called to love our enemies! And to love like our Father loves us all, his beloved children. And we are summoned to take up our cross and be willing to lay our life on the line for our God—obeying God's commands for justice, for the poor, for life without harm, resistance to evil and mercy for all. All this takes a community that is bound stronger than any blood-family in the waters of baptism, the Word of God and the bread that sustains us for this work and enduring grace of life. And God's mercy is wide and God's generosity is deep and true—encompasses the slightest thing, like a cup of water and harder things like the welcome of a prophet who speaks the hard truths. All will know the favor of God—the one who welcomes the just, the prophet and all the little ones (poor and those without power). Love—like a seven-layer cake...down and down and down, sweeter and sweeter as we go.

B THIRTEENTH SUNDAY IN ORDINARY TIME

FIRST READING   Wisdom 1:13–15, 2:23–24
Responsorial Psalm   Psalm 30:2, 4, 5–6, 11–13
SECOND READING   2 Corinthians 8:7, 9, 13–15
GOSPEL   Mark 5:21–43 (or Mark 5:21–24, 35b–43)

We hear that our God rejoices only in life, creation and justice, and that we were created in his image to be imperishable. We must remember this in the midst of evil, injustice and violence. And we must endeavor to live with charity, relieving others, in imitation of the poor man Jesus, sharing with others as a community. Jesus is the Lord of life, bringing the daughter of Jarius back from the dead, and healing the woman who had been excluded (made dead) in her community for twelve years. We are his community commanded to be a place of life, healing, medical care, nourishment for others here now.

C THIRTEENTH SUNDAY IN ORDINARY TIME

FIRST READING   1 Kings 19:16b, 19–21
Responsorial Psalm   Psalm 16:1–2, 5, 7–8, 9–10, 11
SECOND READING   Galatians 5:1, 13–18
GOSPEL   Luke 9:51–62

Elijah anoints Elisha and the mantle/power and burden of prophecy passes on. He calls him at work in the fields. He immediately gives away everything to the people and kisses his father and mother goodbye. He is God's now. And we too have been called to live in this freedom, bound to God, living at the service of others. We are to live under the Spirit that was given to us, more surely and powerfully than even the double portion of Spirit that was given to Elisha.

Jesus is on his way to Jerusalem and he sends his messengers before him—prophets like him to prepare the way. In a Samaritan town they are not welcomed because he was going to Jerusalem (they disagreed with the Jews on the place where God is worshipped. The disciples want to call down destruction on them but Jesus instead reprimand the disciples, who have so little understanding of what it means to follow Jesus to the cross. He tells them that he has nothing, no one, only God. Do we follow the Lord? What do we need to let go of now?

A   FOURTEENTH SUNDAY IN ORDINARY TIME

FIRST READING   Zechariah 9:9–10
Responsorial Psalm   Psalm 145:1–2, 8–9, 10–11, 13–14
SECOND READING   Romans 8:9, 11–13
GOSPEL   Matthew 11:25–30

Jesus is experiencing rejection and hostility from the religious leaders and he seeks to warn his followers that they too will know rejection and imprisonment and persecution from religious people—they will be like their Master, but they are not to be afraid. God is careful of the least, even sparrows, birds without number that are considered nuisances by many but not even one of them is lost without God's awareness. Every hair on our heads has been counted—our God is careful of every one of us and holds each of us dear. We are to only be afraid of those who can bring us to betray our relationships and belief in Jesus and turn from obedience—we are to fear no one else for our God holds us close.

B   FOURTEENTH SUNDAY IN ORDINARY TIME

FIRST READING   Ezekiel 2:2–5
Responsorial Psalm   Psalm 123:1–2, 2, 3–4
SECOND READING   2 Corinthians 12:7–10
GOSPEL   Mark 6:1–6

Now Ezekiel is stood up on his feet and sent to the rebels of Israel. They are hard of face and heart and yet, they will know that a prophet has been sent to confront them with the Word of God. And we, are we rebels? How are we doing, like Paul with the thorns in our flesh that remind us that we are far from being the holy ones of God. Are we ever persecuted for doing justice or speaking the truth? Do we even hear the prophets today or shun them and mock them as the Jesus' hometown did to him? Are there miracles among us, or are there few because there is no Word of God among us? These days, it's time to soften our faces and hearts and listen to God's Word.

C   FOURTEENTH SUNDAY IN ORDINARY TIME

FIRST READING   Isaiah 66:10–14c
Responsorial Psalm   Psalm 66:1–3, 4–5, 6–7, 16, 20
SECOND READING   Galatians 6:14–18
GOSPEL   Luke 10:1–12, 17–20

It is Ordinary Time and rejoicing must be a part of our lives—remembering and taking to heart all that God has done for us, comforting us and providing for us so that we flourish and know his power at work in us and the world. We have been given even God's beloved child and we are baptized and live in the power of the cross and resurrection—we are made utterly new. Do we boast of our marks of being a Christian? Have we ever suffered for what we believe? Have we shared of the excess that is ours? Do we dwell in peace and mercy so that others know that our boasting in the Lord is legimate?

Jesus sends us out two by two to go before him into the world. We are to go lightly, with only what we need, remembering that we are the peacemakers in a world where people destroy those who do not belong to them. We bring peace as the Good News of God. And what are the fruits of peace: healing, welcome, sharing. Always we are to be intimations of what is coming— the reign of God's peace with abiding justice for all. We must keep in mind that it is a privilege and an honor to live in the kingdom now and be a part of Jesus' mission to make holy the whole world.

A   FIFTEENTH SUNDAY IN ORDINARY TIME

FIRST READING   Isaiah 55:10–11
Responsorial Psalm   Psalm 65:10, 11, 12–13–14
SECOND READING   Romans 8:18–23
GOSPEL   Matthew 13:1–23 (or Matthew 13:1–9)

Jesus sits and teaches the crowds by the lake. He talks of seed sown, broadside that falls everywhere: on the path that's eaten by birds, among thin soil and hard ground where it was sorched and among thistles where it's choked and finally in the field and there are crops—some one hundred fold, some sixty, others thirty! What a story! What potent seed! To produce such a crop—even thirty fold is massive returns—imagine an investment with a thirty fold return in one year! Let alone one hundred! But where it falls, what the ground of hearts is like, makes a lot of difference. Even the birds will at least take it and drop it somewhere else. Some of us will sprout and sag. Others of us will not last without a lot of coddling. And even in a field, with a community where the Word is meant to fall—there will be a wide-spread spectrum of food for others—justice, bread, hope, life. How is our field doing? What are we coming up with when the seed of the Word of God is sown among us—only on Sunday—very thin. It needs to be sown liberally weekly in small groups and nurtured for conversion and harvest.

B   FIFTEENTH SUNDAY IN ORDINARY TIME

FIRST READING   Amos 7:12–15
Responsorial Psalm   Psalm 85:9–10, 11–12, 13–14
SECOND READING   Ephesians 1:3–14
                                              (or Ephesians 1:3–10
GOSPEL   Mark 6:7–13

Amos is rejected by the priests and he claims he was only a shepherd. But it is the Lord who took him from his flock and sent him to God's people. God's word is his reason/meaning and power base. We too have been chosen by God. In Jesus

Christ, in our baptisms, to live the wisdom of understanding of the mystery of God's Word and to bring all to communion in Christ. This is why we were sealed in the Spirit. And Jesus sends us forth to live this as a radical sign of the presence of God in the world. We are to go two by two, go with only what we need for the day and live on the hospitality of others and preach repentance. No matter who we are we are always in need of repentance and that is the vow of our baptisms: to live always more in imitation of Jesus' obedience to God.

C FIFTEENTH SUNDAY IN ORDINARY TIME

FIRST READING   Deuteronomy 30:10–14
Responsorial Psalm   Psalm 69:14, 17, 30–31, 33–34, 36, 37
SECOND READING   Colossians 1:15–20
GOSPEL   Luke 10:25–37

Moses pleads with the people to heed God's voice and keep his commandments/law and return with all their heart and soul. He tells them that God's command, his Word, is so close to them, in their mouths and hearts—all they have to do is carry it out. This Word in its fullness we know to be Christ Jesus the image of the invisible God, This Jesus has reconciled both heaven and earth, and all of us to God. We now live in peace that has been shared with us through the cross of Christ, Jesus' obedience in the face of violence and hate.

Jesus is approached by a lawyer and is asked, "What shall I do to receive eternal life? The man should know the answer to his own question. Is he mocking Jesus? He repeats the law but when he is told to obey it, he wants specifics—who is my neighbor? He wants the bottom line, the least he has to do to have eternal life. Jesus tells the story of the Samaritan, hated by the Jews who acts towards a Jew with tenderness and devotion that goes beyond anything required—and he is an enemy! Jesus takes the Samaritan and tells the Jew to imitate him—for he reveals the goodness of God so clearly. This is eternal life—to live with such love and care towards ones' enemies because of pity like God has pity on us. Who are our enemies and are we tending to them in this way as commanded?

A   SIXTEENTH SUNDAY IN ORDINARY TIME

FIRST READING — Wisdom 12:13, 16–19
Responsorial Psalm — Psalm 86:5–6, 9–10, 15–16
SECOND READING — Romans 8:26–27
GOSPEL — Matthew 13:24–43
(or Matthew 13:24–30)

Jesus tells stories about what he is doing and the response of people: a man sows good seed (the Word of God) in a field and while everyone sleeps, an enemy comes and sows weed among the wheat and leaves. They come up together and the servants want to rip out the weeds. They are stopped—they are allowed to grow together until the harvest when the weeds are taken out and burned and the grain harvested. This is the way of the world and we must live together in the field. But the Word of the Kingdom is like a mustard seed—tiny but potent and it grows into a small tree and the birds of the air find rest and shelter in its branches—the kingdom is uncontrollable and the poor of the world will find sanctuary in its tree of life. A woman (God) buries yeast in massive amounts of flour and with hard work of the Spirit and believers the mess rises! Bread for the world—justice, hope and sharing of resources. Parables are stories with infinite meanings. Jesus is the parable of God, a rich source of knowledge about God.

B   SIXTEENTH SUNDAY IN ORDINARY TIME

FIRST READING — Jeremiah 23:1–6
Responsorial Psalm — Psalm 23:1–3, 3–4, 5, 6
SECOND READING — Ephesians 2:13–18
GOSPEL — Mark 6:30–34

Jeremiah tears into the bad shepherds of Israel who care nothing for the people they are supposed to protect, lead and serve. They scatter the sheep, but there will come one who will gather, and increase the flock and abide with them so that they do not know fear or lack, and none will go missing. There will be a righteous shoot and his name will be justice. Jesus is our justice. In him we have been brought back home. He is peace, reconciling us to God and one another, and in the Spirit we are as close to the Father as Jesus is! Jesus today bring us to an out-of-the-way place and rests with us. Jesus and his disciples leave in a boat but people are so desperate for this abiding place of refuge they find in Jesus that they cut them off in their retreat. Jesus is the good shepherd and in pity, he goes to the crowd. With the disciples have we learned such pity and spend time with those who are most in need?

C SIXTEENTH SUNDAY IN ORDINARY TIME

FIRST READING — Genesis 18:1–10a
Responsorial Psalm — Psalm 15:2–3, 3–4, 5
SECOND READING — Colossians 1:24–28
GOSPEL — Luke 10:38–42

Abraham is visited by three men while he is praying—with the presence of Yahweh, the Holy. He seeks to welcome them, wash their feet, feed them and give them hospitality as they rest in the desert. He has the best prepared for them. And as they eat, they ask after Sarah, his wife. He indicates that his wife is there and so that she can hear, they tell them that they will have a son. The promise given is coming to birth.

Our ancestors in faith waited and hoped, and struggled with the Word of God. We too must struggle with our share of the burden of the Gospel and filling up what is lacking in the sufferings of Christ. We must seek to make known to all the world the mystery that we know in our bodies. If we proclaim Christ, it is Christ crucified and risen. Jesus is welcomed into the home of Mary and Martha (and Lazarus). Martha tends to his needs, (as did Abraham and Sarah) and Mary sits at his feet, listening to his words. Martha wants help from Mary, but Jesus defends Mary who listens/obeys the Word. [These are the last lines of the chapter with the story of the Good Samaritan and the lawyer immediately preceeding it. This piece cannot be understood without that one—"only one thing is needed. Mary has chosen the better part" follows upon the Good Samaritan taking care of the man left for dead in the ditch. The better part, the one thing needed is to attend to those who are left for dead—as Jesus will be—and to see the face of God in one's enemy. All else pales in comparison.]

A SEVENTEENTH SUNDAY IN ORDINARY TIME

FIRST READING   1 Kings 3:5, 7–12
Responsorial Psalm   Psalm 119:57, 72, 76–77, 127, 128, 129–130
SECOND READING   Romans 8:28–30
GOSPEL   Matthew 13:44–52

More marvelous stories. A man finds a treasure hidden in a field. How? And he buries it again. Why? Sells all that he has and buys the field. And rejoices! What about us? Most of us would consider it 'finders keepers' and take the treasure and run. What's the treasure? The word of God, the kingdom of the poor and just, the presence of the Risen Lord, our relationship with the Father, in Jesus, by the power of the Spirit—all of these! But you can't have the treasure alone—you have to have the community (the field) as well. And nothing else matters—it brings such joy to share it with others. The story of the pearl of great price found! Again joy! Sell everything (give to the poor and lay up treasure in heaven!) and what do you do with one pearl? Make a ring out of it—or find others to string together on a necklace (all the stories of God strung together)...or better still sell it again to bring joy to the poor. These are all the meanings, and they are just the first layers. Dig, look—don't take for yourself. Share the Word together and find the treasure that has been given to others!

B SEVENTEENTH SUNDAY IN ORDINARY TIME

FIRST READING   2 Kings 4:42–44
Responsorial Psalm   Psalm 145:10–11, 15–16, 17–18
SECOND READING   Ephesians 4:1–6
GOSPEL   John 6:1–15

Elisha takes a gift of twenty barley loaves (the bread of the poor) and with it feeds a hundred and still there are leftovers. Paul in jail pleads that his community stays at peace, in unity, remembering that God is in all and that all in one in God. And Jesus seeks to share this peace, this feast, this communion with the masses of people who come to him in need. The disciples are dismayed by the crowd's size but there is a young child who brings 5 loaves and a couple of fish. Jesus takes the gift, shares it, modeling what we are to do and there is enough left over to feed a world (12 baskets, all of Israel). The breaking of Word and Bread is our unity but it is meant to be made reality, by feeding the world with the excess that is always shared with us by our God with us.

C SEVENTEENTH SUNDAY IN ORDINARY TIME

FIRST READING   Genesis 18:20–32
Responsorial Psalm   Psalm 138:1–2, 2–3, 6–7, 7–8
SECOND READING   Colossians 2:12–14
GOSPEL   Luke 11:1–13

We hear the story of the intended destruction of Sodom and Gomorrah because of their evil. But Abraham pleads on their behalf. Save the city for the sake of the just that dwell there as well...if only there are 50, 40,30,20...even 10 and God agrees. And what of our cities, with our economies, how we treat immigrants, strangers, the poor and the homeless, the callousness of our budgets and laws—are there even 10 just ones among us that might save us—are we pleading on behalf of other places?

We are alive in Christ, dead to sin. The cross has been our lifeline and root. Jesus teaches us to pray, as we live in him, to the glory of God. We are all one, with one Father and we seek to worship God's name and bring the kingdom of God—of mercy, justice, charity, reconciliation and at-one-ment, with no harm to anyone in need. We ask to provide for everyone's need for today, sharing of our abundance while trusting in our Father. We ask for mercy and give it always, everywhere, to everyone. We ask for courage to stand fast in the face of difficulty and temptation and to stand faithful even at our dying. When we pray we must attend to God with trust, with confidence and knowing he is our Father. And if we must ask, ask for the Spirit that binds us all as one in God.

A EIGHTEENTH SUNDAY IN ORDINARY TIME

FIRST READING   Isaiah 55:1–3
Responsorial Psalm   Psalm 145:8–9, 15–16, 17–18
SECOND READING   Romans 8:35, 37–39
GOSPEL   Matthew 14:13–21

❋ John has been beheaded and when Jesus hears the violent news he goes to a secluded place but the people hear of the news and are devastated—now he goes looking for Jesus and Jesus turns his face towards them in compassion and turns towards the cross and his own violent death. He heals them, touches them, teaches them, his presence comforting and strengthening them and then it grows late and they need food. Jesus takes his disciples' food and has them give it away to the crowds after having blessed it and broken it apart and shared it around. The disciples' food is taken from them and their job is to distribute their food and to collect the leftovers. And the leftovers fill twelve baskets. Where did the baskets come from? The miracle was the sharing of all the peoples' food—and people eating together who would never have thought to break bread as one. And it's a huge crowd—five hundred men (ratio of women and children to men is five or six to one so it's about twenty-five thousand to thirty thousand—the new Passover, exodus, covenant and Eucharist). Jesus begins the way that will lead to death—the way of compassion, of healing and feeding the world, his presence, his Word, his bread and his justice.

C EIGHTEENTH SUNDAY IN ORDINARY TIME

FIRST READING   Ecclesiastes 1:2; 2:21–23
Responsorial Psalm   Psalm 90:3–4, 5–6, 12–13, 14, 17
SECOND READING   Colossians 3:1–5, 9–11
GOSPEL   Luke 12:13–21

❋ We hear wisdom from the era of Solomon—folk wisdom that is common-sense for masses of people. It is rather pessimistic—seeing all our days as sorrow and grief and never finding rest. But we do not believe that or succumb to such despair for we have been raised up with Christ in our baptisms and the Lord intercedes for us at the right hand of the Father. We are to put to death in us whatever hinders us from living in Christ—we are to be new men and women, formed anew in the image of Christ.

Jesus is asked to settle a family dispute over inheritance. But he refuses and says clearly: "Avoid greed in all its forms." He tells them the parable of someone who has so much that he has no place to put it, pulls down the old barns and builds bigger and bigger, planning what he is going to do with all his extra wealth and holdings. But he lives without thought, without sharing (he would have been despised in the Jewish community) and he lives without offering to God, or an attitude of thankfulness. He will die that night. This is the way with those who do not know how to grow rich in the sight of God—by sharing with the poor, by working for justice, by giving thanks to God by giving away one's excess—and then giving with ever greater generosity. Where do we stand this day, this night before God?

A NINETEENTH SUNDAY IN ORDINARY TIME

FIRST READING   1 Kings 19:9a, 11–13a
Responsorial Psalm   Psalm 85:9, 10, 11–12, 13–14
SECOND READING   Romans 9:1–5
GOSPEL   Matthew 14:22–33

Jesus sends his disciples away in the boat and leaves to pray. He is alone. They are out on the open sea and caught in a maelstrom. At dawn Jesus comes to them walking on water. Images of dawn, resurrection, life beyond anything we can know here. And they are terrified. But Peter climbs out and heads towards Jesus. He doesn't last long on his own, begins to sink into the waters. The waters of baptism, to die with Christ so that he can live with him. He has begun to reject Jesus' call to the cross and death and will continue to do so until after the resurrection. He has started out strong, grown fearful and cries out to Jesus to save him. He is a 'man of little faith', this man who will lead the church one day. Are we men and women of little faith, easily terrified, lacking in belief in the power and presence of our God in history, always? They end with "You are the Son of God." This title is both revelatory of the greatest of the prophets and those who had the Word of God in their mouths. But they have no real sense of who Jesus is—The Word of God made flesh among us; God incarnated, living, dying and rising with us. Do we know our God?

B   NINETEENTH SUNDAY IN ORDINARY TIME

FIRST READING   1 Kings 19:4–8
Responsorial Psalm   Psalm 34:2–3, 4–5, 6–7, 8–9
SECOND READING   Ephesians 4:30—5:2
GOSPEL   John 6:41–51

✦ Elijah is disheartened and wants to die, but an angel comes to him and feeds him again and again so that he can make his journey to Horeb, the mountain of God. Today we are told to be sure to do nothing to sadden the Spirit and rid ourselves of bitterness, anger, harsh words, slander and malice and imitate God in loving each other. Jesus feeds us the bread of life that sustains us daily, that is the bread of justice, of hope and freedom, to be shared around with all. We are fed food that enables us to live forever and to live even now as those taught by God (Scripture) and with Jesus' own life (Eucharist). We do not dare despair or grow weary. We are sustained.

C   NINETEENTH SUNDAY IN ORDINARY TIME

FIRST READING   Wisdom 18:6–9
Responsorial Psalm   Psalm 33:1, 12, 18–19, 20–22
SECOND READING   Hebrews 11:1–2, 8–19
GOSPEL   Luke 12:35–40

✦ Are we wise? Are we the holy children of the good who offer sacrifice in secret who live and wait with courage? Are we faithful like our ancestors who died in faith? We have been given what they staked their lives on, but do we live with intensity and devotion to sharing the riches that are ours. Luke tells us how we are to live—by sharing with the poor and putting our treasure there in God's kingdom of justice/peace and forgiveness now.

We must live with watchfulness so that if today our God returns then we are not only ready, we are delighted. We are servants of God, like the beloved servant-son Jesus and by our baptisms we commit ourselves to doing Jesus' work now in the world. So much has been given to us—are we thankful and do we share it in gratitude, giving it away with joy?

A TWENTIETH SUNDAY IN ORDINARY TIME

FIRST READING	Isaiah 56:1, 6–7
Responsorial Psalm	Psalm 67:2–3, 5, 6, 8
SECOND READING	Romans 11:13–15, 29–32
GOSPEL	Matthew 15:21–28

This is a benchmark in Matthew's gospel—Jesus has turned away from his own people, from Israel and its leaders, all of whom are rejecting him and the call to the good news to the poor, and the cross. He leaves and in gentile territory is hounded by a Canaanite woman crying out in distress, desperate for her daughter's healing. Jesus doesn't initially respond and his disciples are cold-hearted. He has come to the lost sheep of the house of Israel, not the dogs of other countries who do not even believe in Yahweh. But she is persistent and sharp, saying in humility she'll take what the sheep, the children have thrown under the table for the dogs. Jesus is taken aback—this is faith unlike any in Israel. Her daughter is healed and Jesus is sent to a larger horizon—to bring the good news to the whole world. What a gift she gave him as he gifted her. This is what we are all called to do: to fill up what is lacking in one another by the power of the Spirit of God.

B TWENTIETH SUNDAY IN ORDINARY TIME

FIRST READING	Proverbs 9:1–6
Responsorial Psalm	Psalm 34:2–3, 10–11, 12–13, 14–15
SECOND READING	Ephesians 5:15–20
GOSPEL	John 6:51–58

Meet Wisdom! Look for understanding, forsake foolishness and enter the house of God. Are we wise or foolish in our behavior. Are we ignorant or do we discern the will of God (Scriptures) Do we worship God with others in public, giving thanks, and making sure that we worship God in fact and in reality too? We come together to be fed with God's own life: Word and Bread/flesh and Wine/blood and this food makes us wise. If we eat and absorb this life, live this life now, we will one day know God's life and wisdom in its fullness.

C TWENTIETH SUNDAY IN ORDINARY TIME

FIRST READING   Jeremiah 38:4–6, 8–10
Responsorial Psalm   Psalm 40:2, 3, 4, 18
SECOND READING   Hebrews 12:1–4
GOSPEL   Luke 12:49–53

Jeremiah is assailed by his own countrymen because he demoralizes the remaining soldiers and people left in the city. (They are under siege because they did not rely on the power of God, but made pacts with other nations that are now over-running them). The king lets them do what they want and Jeremiah is thrown into a cistern where he sinks in the mud. This is the end of a prophet, or an interim. The king is approached by a Cushite and they are allowed to haul Jeremiah out before he dies. A true prophet tells the people what is reality, what is happening and why. But people do not want to hear it. There are only two choices with a prophet: hear and obey, or refuse to listen and attack the prophet.

And it is the same for all the followers of Jesus, the great cloud of witnesses who has gone before us, running the race, and even enduring shame and death with Jesus who brings fire and light upon the earth. We are not to break in the face of opposition or grow despondent, but face the divisions and difficulties that being faithful to God entails. In this Ordinary Time we are called to look at the depth of our commitment and whether we are speaking truly in a world that is in opposition to the Gospel of Jesus.

A TWENTY-FIRST SUNDAY IN ORDINARY TIME

FIRST READING — Isaiah 22:19–23
Responsorial Psalm — Psalm 138:1–2, 2–3, 6-8
SECOND READING — Romans 11:33–36
GOSPEL — Matthew 16:13–20

✺ Again and again we are questioned: who do we think Jesus is? Is he our personal friend, teacher, model? Is he a prophet like those gone before in the tradition calling the people back to justice, to pity for the poor and the only worship that God desires—wholehearted devotion to obedience to the Word of God? Is he the beloved Son of God—something each of us must learn from the Father, in the power of the Spirit in our baptisms? Are we truly members of the Body, the Church that stands for the truth in public no matter what is happening in history and forgives, yet holds bound those who do evil publicly too? Are we built on the rock of forgiveness and telling the truth as we work for justice and the kingdom of God's peace in the world? Our God must forever be larger than our small petitions and we must grow in our public witness, like the prophets we are made by baptism and confirmation. What Word do we speak because we belong to the Word made flesh?

B TWENTY-FIRST SUNDAY IN ORDINARY TIME

FIRST READING — Joshua 24:1–2a, 15–17, 18b
Responsorial Psalm — Psalm 34:2–3, 16–17, 18–19, 20–21, 22–23
SECOND READING — Ephesians 5:21–32
(or Ephesians 5:2, 25–32)
GOSPEL — John 6:60–69

✺ Joshua calls the people together and ritually demands to know where they stand before God. And the people proclaim that they will serve the Lord God as their ancestors were called to serve, when brought out of Egypt into freedom. And we are to obey the Lord. Married couples are to obey the Lord and to love one another as God as loved all of us. Each submits first to Christ and together to Christ. Jesus' words are Spirit and life and yet there are many who leave Jesus because of his words. When asked why he stays, Simon Peter proclaims that they all have come to believe that Jesus is God's Holy One. Have we all come to believe that and do we obey and serve God alone, in Jesus' Body here on earth or have we submitted ourselves to others?

C TWENTY-FIRST SUNDAY IN ORDINARY TIME

FIRST READING   Isaiah 66:18–21
Responsorial Psalm   Psalm 117:1, 2
SECOND READING   Hebrews 12:5–7, 11–13
GOSPEL   Luke 13:22–30

Isaiah sings of the gathering of the nations and of every language and send messengers to the far coastlands so that all may hear and see the glory of the Lord God—from the greatest who travel in chariots to the least who come on mules and in carts or on foot. And all will be gathered, together to worship God. God's hope and prayer is that all the nations and peoples of the world will be united—that is the worship that God wants.

Paul is writing to his people who are experiencing hardships and persecution is mounting against Christians. Discipline is the school for disciples—becoming like our master, the poor man, the crucified one, obedient to God and so rejected by many and murdered. Yet God attests to this discipline and practice and raised Jesus to life. Jesus goes his way calling people to come after him and it is a narrow way—the gate of compassion, sharing with the poor (remember Lazarus/Dives and all that happens at gates—the widow of Naim). It is not being in and eating in the company of Jesus that will necessarily make us true disciples but whether or not we serve the least and follow humbly after our Lord.

A TWENTY-SECOND SUNDAY IN ORDINARY TIME

FIRST READING — Jeremiah 20:7–9
Responsorial Psalm — Psalm 63:2, 3–4, 5–6, 8–9
SECOND READING — Romans 12:1–2
GOSPEL — Matthew 16:21–27

We must hear again Jesus trying to make clear to his disciples that he is going to Jerusalem and there he will be rejected, suffer many things, be murdered and rise again. And Peter, though they all feel the same way, reproaches Jesus and tries to take him aside and basically tell him to shut up and stop saying those things. He's frightening them and discouraging them. Jesus is clear: Peter is a stumbling block, a rock getting in the way of God's will and the way of the cross and the Resurrection. He's thinking like the world, not like God. Jesus is the Son of Man, not a worldly king and his ways are drastically different than the power bases of kings, governments and armies and nations. His power is revealed in suffering, in resistance to evil that does no harm to others and in forgiveness and mercy even for enemies as well as for friends who betray and desert him. Each will have to decide whether to stand with Jesus or against him. We must decide with every event of the world, every decision, relationship and circumstance. Are we stumbling blocks to the coming of justice and peace—God's way in the world?

B TWENTY-SECOND SUNDAY IN ORDINARY TIME

FIRST READING — Deuteronomy 4:1–2, 6–8
Responsorial Psalm — Psalm 15:2–3, 3–4, 4–5
SECOND READING — James 1:17–18, 21b–22, 27
GOSPEL — Mark 7:1–8, 14–15, 21–23

Moses exhorts the people to observe the law, to obey them and set their sights by them so that they will be seen as a wise and intelligent people, whose God is close to them. The whole law is set before them. And we have been given the whole law/wisdom and gift of God in Jesus. God wills to bring us to birth with a word spoken in truth and to take that Word down to our roots. We're supposed to care for the least and worship with integrity. In the words of Jesus in the gospel we are to do no evil and render obedience to God from deep in our hearts. Do we heed God's commandments or are we more intent on human traditions and what others think of us? Again we are questioned before Jesus.

C TWENTY-SECOND SUNDAY IN ORDINARY TIME

FIRST READING — Sirach 3:17–18, 20, 28–29
Responsorial Psalm — Psalm 68:4–5, 6–7, 10–11
SECOND READING — Hebrews 12:18–19, 22–24a
GOSPEL — Luke 14:1, 7–14

We are told to be humble, and to listen (meaning to obey) and to give alms generously because they atone for sin. Basic human advice that is useful to all people. We however, have drawn near to God in Jesus (not fire, mountains, darkness and storm as theophanies of old). We have come close to the community that believes in the Risen Lord, the Word made flesh. We are the honored and beloved children of God at the banquet table of the kingdom of justice, peace and mercy for all.

Jesus' story tells us how we are to live, with humility, not putting ourselves first, and not making sure that we are in the places of honor and are acknowledged in public for what we do or who we are. We are to be among the least, to serve, eat with and dwell among those at the bottom. And we are to invite and make friends with those no one remembers to invite to the feast of the Lord and to a life of abundance and justice. We should be pleased to do as much as we can for those who cannot repay us (that is the way we are with God!)

A TWENTY-THIRD SUNDAY IN ORDINARY TIME

FIRST READING — Ezekiel 33:7–9
Responsorial Psalm — Psalm 95:1–2, 6–7, 8–9
SECOND READING — Romans 13:8–10
GOSPEL — Matthew 18:15–20

✴ Jesus returns to the core and heart of his good news: forgiveness and reconciliation. This is a primer on how to do it, when it's difficult and the other will not entertain the idea of needing to be forgiven. First in private, one on one. Then with one or two others, neutral parties as witnesses; then to a small assembly and then: treat them like a publican. But that's the rub! How does Jesus treat the public sinner? With more compassion, understanding and more forgiveness and love. This is love in practice; not to shun them or exclude them but still forgive and seek to reconcile—this is love unto death, or love as I have loved you. And the next thing to do is pray for reconciliation—the second phase of forgiveness and healing in the body of Christ. This should be the core and heart of our prayers in public—the reconciling of all enemies, of all nations and all the world. What do we pray for when we gather?

B TWENTY-THIRD SUNDAY IN ORDINARY TIME

FIRST READING	Isaiah 35:4–7a
Responsorial Psalm	Psalm 146:7, 8–9, 9–10
SECOND READING	James 2:1–5
GOSPEL	Mark 7:31–37

✴ Have courage, do not fear, see, your God comes, demanding justice! Do we see and hear the demands and saving power of our God? Do we see that God chooses the poor and the powerless in this world to reveal and inherit the kingdom and faith? We have been taken from the crowd like the deaf man and our ears have been opened and we have been commanded to be still, to shut up until we know the God who has come to us and given us sight and hearing. We are to listen to the Word of God and let it take root under our tongues. But once it is done and we are baptized, are we more than just a story to tell, a report spread around? Are we the Word of God demanding and bringing justice to all?

C TWENTY-THIRD SUNDAY IN ORDINARY TIME

FIRST READING   Wisdom 9:13–18b
Responsorial Psalm   Psalm 90:3–4, 5–6, 12–13, 14–17
SECOND READING   Philemon 9–10, 12–17
GOSPEL   Luke 14:25–33

❋ Who knows God's wisdom and counsel? Mortals just guess and plan. They are timid and unsure but God gives his wisdom and sends his Spirit to help make straight the paths of all on earth. Paul writes to Philemon about his runaway slave, whom Paul calls 'my heart'. Paul sends the slave back to Philemon. The slave is now a believer, a member of the Body of Christ, a brother, a beloved. This is the wisdom of God that breaks the hold of slavery, of servitude for all who call themselves Christians, followers of Christ. Paul is adept at getting Philemon to look at his slave as a new person in Christ and he must come to know him not as a slave, but as a man and in the Lord. It is appalling that even with all the Words of Jesus and writings such as this that slavery was practiced and never questioned by Christians for nearly 2 centuries after the Incarnation and still is practiced in so many parts of the world.

Jesus calls us to come after him, to leave family and loved ones, even ourselves (to put on Christ and belong to the sisters, brothers and mothers that hear the Word and obey). We are called to take up our cross—the burden of the gospel and what is laid on us as suffering because we preach and practice the gospel in the world. Have we considered what we have been baptized into—the lifelong following of Jesus to the cross and the building of a kingdom at odds with the world, because ours is built of love, justice, forgiveness, mercy, non-violence and peace?

A TWENTY-FOURTH SUNDAY IN ORDINARY TIME

FIRST READING   Sirach 27:30—28:7
Responsorial Psalm   Psalm 103:1–2, 3–4, 9–10, 11–12
SECOND READING   Romans 14:7–9
GOSPEL   Matthew 18:21–35

Again and again in this season of Ordinary Time we hear it again: how many times do I have to forgive? The words are in Peter's mouth as the head of the disciples and the spokesperson for the church but it is each our own question. And the story that Jesus tells is both comforting and harsh, filled with both mercy and just due demanding that we look to our own lives and see what we are doing to one another—and so, what our Father will do with us. We are forgiven a debt that is impossible to forgive. This is God's mercy in Jesus. And then do we go out and choke the life out of others demanding that they immediately compensate for what we think they have done to us? It is the other servants who are distressed and who go to the king—do we often distress the other members of our community by our cold-heartedness and lack of compassion, and lack of justice—that we forgive as we have been forgiven? How sincerely do we practice Jesus' word?

B   TWENTY-FOURTH SUNDAY IN ORDINARY TIME

FIRST READING — Isaiah 50:5–9a
Responsorial Psalm — Psalm 116:1–2, 3–4, 5–6, 8–9
SECOND READING — James 2:14–18
GOSPEL — Mark 8:27–35

Do we imitate the disciple of God: Jesus? It is time to open our ears to God, to stand and offer our lives on behalf of others without violence, no matter what we experience, and we are not to despair, relying on God's presence/nearness. Our lives must mirror our words: blessing, and blessings made reality by our care for those in need: those hungry, cold, without shelter or security. Faith is useless without practice. We must remember that we follow the servant of God, brought down to being the least among us by rejection, torture and death. Are we anything like the One we profess to follow: the Servant of all?

C   TWENTY-FOURTH SUNDAY IN ORDINARY TIME

FIRST READING   Exodus 32:7–11, 13–14
Responsorial Psalm   Psalm 51:3–4, 12–13, 17, 19
SECOND READING   1 Timothy 1:12–17
GOSPEL   Luke 15:1–32

The people have renounced God and in their depravity worship an idol they made, from the idols of Egypt that enslaved them. Moses implores the mercy and great power of God on behalf of his people once again and, as though he is just waiting to be asked, he relents and does them no harm. Paul writes to Timothy telling him of his past evil, his sin, and violence against others. He also tells Timothy what God has done for him in making him his servant, in his mercy. This too, is our situation no matter who we are—it is God's mercy that has sustained us and transformed us and made us holy/good.

Jesus tells three stories, all about the mercy of God, forgiveness and trying to keep the sheep together. The lost sheep that strays, he goes after, leaving the others to fend for themselves (take care of each other). The woman loses a coin (part of her dowry) and searches for it to put it back on her belt that she wears. And the father wishes both his sons would recognize his own love for them and in mercy to forgive one another and come back together as brothers. We are all the beloved of God and our relationships with God the Father are only as good as our relationships with each other. Do we live in such a way that we nurture and strengthen the communion of the Church and all peoples?

A   TWENTY-FIFTH SUNDAY IN ORDINARY TIME

FIRST READING   Isaiah 55:6–9
Responsorial Psalm   Psalm 145:2–3, 8–9, 17–18
SECOND READING   Philippians 1:20c–24, 27
GOSPEL   Matthew 20:1–16a

Oh, that story of the vineyard. Some work all day, some nine hours, others four or some barely at all and the foreman comes

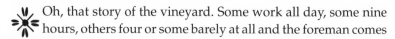

out and pays everyone the usual daily wage, on orders from the vineyard owner. Some are overjoyed, stunned, grateful, knowing they never could have worked for the usual wage (because of being old, sick, pregnant, handicapped, outsider, new to the group, etc.) and others are furious and indignant that others are treated with the same respect and dignity that they are—they worked for their pay, not like those people. This is Jesus' and the Father's kingdom and it's not like the way the world operates where the principles of usefulness, greed and self-promotion rule. Not here! The least are taken care of first and all the others wait on them so that they can be reminded of both the compassion and justice of our God and that we are all his beloved children living on the graciousness of our Father. Have we forgotten? Did we ever learn? Or does the mercy and kindness of our God, the words of good news to the poor and the call to practice this kind of economics make us annoyed, or furious?

B TWENTY-FIFTH SUNDAY IN ORDINARY TIME

FIRST READING — Wisdom 2:12, 17–20
Responsorial Psalm — Psalm 54:3–4, 5, 6–8
SECOND READING — James 3:16—4:3
GOSPEL — Mark 9:30–37

Are we aligned with the wicked of the earth, setting traps for the righteous and those who speak the Word of God to us? Do we ignore the Truth, tormenting those who obviously belong to God, and do we shame them, and kill them? And do we do it among ourselves: with jealousy, ambition, discord and evil? Or simply put, are we born of God and are we the peacemakers, acting with wisdom and compassion, reaping justice? Again we are invited to be children of God, like Jesus with his Father's arms wrapped around him, in suffering and death, servants and the least among those on earth. It does sound like Lent and it is time for us to relent and turn towards the Truth of God in Jesus.

C TWENTY-FIFTH SUNDAY IN ORDINARY TIME

FIRST READING   Amos 8:4–7
Responsorial Psalm   Psalm 113:1–2, 4–6, 7–8
SECOND READING   1 Timothy 2:1–8
GOSPEL   Luke 16:1–13

Amos excoriates the people who destroy the poor and at the same time practice injustice/greed to make a profit, sell the laborer short, endanger peoples' lives and make people no more than indentured servants. Even at worship all they think about is how to make more money, in unjust ways. God will never forget a single thing they have done to the poorest and the least. We are among the richest nations of the earth, by far, and the least generous in giving even when disaster strikes—what does our God see us doing?

These readings declare that we are Christian but that we live in a world that is not and we must reveal our being Christian/ in our words/ deeds / actions. We are not to just singly make do when our nation/country defies God and practices what God finds abhorrent in regard to economic justice, the basic necessities of life for all and life itself with human dignity.

Jesus tells the story of a manager who cheats his master, and at the same time, ingratiates himself with his master's customers/ debtors. He is going to be dismissed (in his greed, he overstepped the profit he took—more than his master's share) and he brings in each of the debtors and substantially drops what they owe (you can see how much he was raking in). Thus he makes friends who will provide for him when he is out of a job. The master recognizes his astuteness and praises him. And us—what have we done with what our God has shared with us? Do we make a profit on the side for ourselves? Can we be trusted with the treasures of God—the poor, the little ones, the crucified ones, those who are the presence of God among us?

A TWENTY-SIXTH SUNDAY IN ORDINARY TIME

FIRST READING　　　　　　　　　　　Ezekiel 18:25–28
Responsorial Psalm　　　　　Psalm 25:4–5, 6–7, 8–9
SECOND READING　　　　　　　Philippians 2:1–11
GOSPEL　　　　　　　　　　　　Matthew 21:28–32

❋ Jesus pushes the Pharisees, but he's also pushing his disciples who are confused and beginning to be afraid to be with Jesus on where they stand and why. He tells the parable of the two sons: the first says "I'll obey" but doesn't and the other says "I won't obey" but does. Which did the father's will? They don't want to answer, but have to acknowledge that actions speak louder than words of religion or pious devotion and practice. Jesus assures them solemnly (as in a judgment on them) that the prostitutes, tax collectors and public sinners whom they despise are getting into the kingdom before they are! That in itself would have been enough to enrage them. But he continues with John's message and life—condemning them because they saw the conversion he called forth in those they excluded from God's mercy and yet they still didn't change their ways. He condemns them for their not listening to John or being converted and sideways for doing the same with him. Do we listen and say "I'll go" but we don't? Have we heard the word and converted our lives?

B TWENTY-SIXTH SUNDAY IN ORDINARY TIME

FIRST READING　　　　　　　　　　　Numbers 11:25–29
Responsorial Psalm　　　Psalm 19:8, 10, 12–13, 14
SECOND READING　　　　　　　　　　James 5:1–6
GOSPEL　　　　　　　　　Mark 9:38–43, 45, 47–48

❋ The Spirit that rested on Moses is shared with seventy others! And Moses' prayer echoes today: "Would that all Yahweh's people were prophet and that he would send his Spirit on all of them!" James is one of those prophets crying justice/judgment upon the rich who are insensitive to the evil they lay on others by their injustice and greed and their part in killing the Word and those who proclaim it without doing violence to anyone. We have been baptized in water, Spirit and the blood of Jesus, summoned to be witnesses with the Crucified One, crying justice in our prayers, words and decisions, being and calling others to be the servants of those destroyed violently and the ransom of those in need. Do we know for a minute what our baptisms initiate us into: the Body of the Lord?

C TWENTY-SIXTH SUNDAY IN ORDINARY TIME

FIRST READING   Amos 6:1a, 4–7
Responsorial Psalm   Psalm 146:7, 8–9, 9–10
SECOND READING   1 Timothy 6:11–16
GOSPEL   Luke 16:19–31

Again Amos goes after the rich, the complacent, those who feast, who live luxuriously, wasting money on clothes, shelter, feasts, pleasures, hedonism. They care nothing about the collapse of Joseph—the poor of the land. So they will be the first to go into exile and know hardship. Their insensitivity and wanton revelry will soon be over. What do we waste billions of dollars on, while the world starves, goes without water, lives in misery and violence? We are called the men and women of God. Do we look like what Timothy has been called to practice and witness to in his world? God gives life to all. Do we make sure that all have life by our faithfulness to God, our steadfastness in everlasting life that we share with others—this is our charge and the way we fulfill our profession of faith—by giving/sharing life with all.

We hear the story of Dives (rich) and Lazarus who is miserably poor. What separates them in their lives/religion is a gate/fence. Lazarus longs for scraps and has only dogs for company and Dives is unaware and cares not for even his own (Jewish countryman). They both die and Lazarus knows the fullness of life and Dives knows only torment. He still does not see Lazarus as a beloved child of God, only a servant to help him out. He cries out to send someone to tell his brothers. But Abraham (father of faith) tells him sternly that his brothers/like him had the prophets to listen to but they didn't. They won't listen to someone who comes back from the dead. Have we listened to the prophets? If we haven't then have we really ever listened to the prophet Jesus who has come back to life?

A TWENTY-SEVENTH SUNDAY IN ORDINARY TIME

FIRST READING   Isaiah 5:1–7
Responsorial Psalm   Psalm 80:9, 12, 13–14, 15–16, 19–20
SECOND READING   Philippians 4:6–9
GOSPEL   Matthew 21:33–43

One of the vineyard stories—where the owner does everything possible to care for the vineyard (the people of Israel) and then sends his servants to collect his share of the grapes for wine. They are insulted, tormented, stoned, killed (the prophets calling the people to justice, worship and care for the poor—God's share of the vineyard and covenant). Finally he sends his own Son and they kill him thinking to take the vineyard for themselves. Judgment follows upon the people and especially upon the leaders and Jesus declares that he is the foundational stone of the covenant and the one long-awaited, but now the promise will be passed to others who will believe and care for the vineyard and it will be the work of the Lord. We believe that we are those people. Do we give our God the first fruits of the vineyard for justice, for the poor and the true worship of God or do we go the way of our ancestors rejecting the prophets, the Word of God and destroying the vineyard or using it for our own greed, selfish purposes and ignoring our call to be wine for the poor, the lost and those who need tending and caring? We too will know judgment—and we have known the 'rock of our salvation' Jesus the Lord.

B TWENTY-SEVENTH SUNDAY IN ORDINARY TIME

FIRST READING   Genesis 2:18–24
Responsorial Psalm   Psalm 128:1–2, 3, 4–5, 6
SECOND READING   Hebrews 2:9–11
GOSPEL   Mark 10:2–16 (or Mark 10:2–12)

✴ We hear one of the stories of the creation: woman created because it was not good for a man to be alone. We are all created for company, to assuage loneliness, to be one flesh, to be one human race. And marriage is the physical way the human race is recreated generation to generation, in a relationship of shared encouragement (shared heart). And we hear of Jesus—lowly as one of us, knowing, life and death, the mercy of God and fullness of life—so that all of us might know the glory of being the children of God, the brothers and sisters of God. God's kin in Jesus is our larger, truer and deeper family, more than any blood tie or marriage as the world plans. God is intent that we all become faithful children in his kingdom, no matter what our choices of vocation. How faithful are we to God's kingdom and mercy?

C TWENTY-SEVENTH SUNDAY IN ORDINARY TIME

FIRST READING   Habakkuk 1:2–3; 2:2–4
Responsorial Psalm   Psalm 95:1–2, 6–7, 8–9
SECOND READING   2 Timothy 1:6–8, 13–14
GOSPEL   Luke 17:5–10

✴ The prophet cries out to God—all there is is violence, ruin, misery and strife. And then Habakkuk is given a vision that he must keep for the vision will come true. We are to wait for it and we are to believe and be just and so, live. What vision do we live by and cling to when there is so much violence and discord in our world and our church? Timothy is told to stir into flame the gift that was given to him—to be strong, loving and wise and never be ashamed to bear his share of the hardship that comes with the gospel.

Do we live by faith, even as small as a mustard seed? Are we the servants of the Lord at work as shepherds (gathering and keeping the church together), plowing (planting and teaching, nourishing the gospel in others) and serving one another at the table of the Lord and in the community's daily needs to survive? Do we remember that we are servants and that we must do as we have been told? And most of us a bit useless, even when we fulfill our duties? Have we ever done all that we are commanded? O God, help us to live by the vision of Jesus and your kingdom among us in the presence of justice and peace.

A TWENTY-EIGHTH SUNDAY IN ORDINARY TIME

FIRST READING · Isaiah 25:6–10a
Responsorial Psalm · Psalm 23:1–3a, 3b–4, 5, 6
SECOND READING · Philippians 4:12–14, 19–20
GOSPEL · Matthew 22:1–10

We hear again of what the kingdom of God is like in the parable of the wedding of the king's son. The guest list is drawn up and the invitations are sent out—but everyone refuses, excusing themselves—other more pressing business, economics, buying and selling, their fields. Not only that, they insult and kill those who invite them (prophets).

Then the soldiers are sent to destroy the city and those who murdered others. Then the invitation goes out to others—anyone on the streets—both good and bad and they are brought in to the feast. The king arrives and moves among the guests, finding one without a garment (they were provided at their entrance into the feast) and when questioned, he is cast out. This is a short history of both covenants/history, culminating with the wedding feast of eucharist now and baptismal life. We are all invited and drawn in—sinners and saints called to eat in the kingdom. We have baptismal garments and we will be judged on how we have worn it throughout our lives, unto death. Do we appreciate the invitation and that we are in the kingdom? Do we live as though we were never brought into the presence of the king's son? We have been called—do we live as those chosen by God to reveal the fullness of the kingdom of justice and peace for the poor, for all?

B TWENTY-EIGHTH SUNDAY IN ORDINARY TIME

FIRST READING · Wisdom 7:7–11
Responsorial Psalm · Psalm 90:12–13, 14–15, 16–17
SECOND READING · Hebrews 4:12–13
GOSPEL · Mark 10:17–30 (or Mark 10:17–27)

✺ Have we prayed for wisdom and understanding wanting it more than anything else? Do we live in the radiance that is Wisdom (Spirit of Jesus)? Wisdom is the Word of God sharper than any two-edged sword, living and effective, severing soul/spirit, joints/marrow, judging intentions/thoughts of the heart. Wisdom is the heart and eye of God that judges us always. Wisdom looks at us with love and says: "There is one more thing you must do." Must do—this is not option. We must go, sell what we have, share it with the poor, then come back and follow Jesus the poor, crucified one. We whine like Peter that we've left everything and what are we going to get? We will be given in return a hundredfold in everything that is essential: the kin of Jesus, community, all that we need shared, intimacy and friendship, even persecution if we are faithful and life everlasting, now and forever. This is wisdom. This is the Word. How wise are we?

C TWENTY-EIGHTH SUNDAY IN ORDINARY TIME

FIRST READING	2 Kings 5:14–17
Responsorial Psalm	Psalm 98:1, 2–3, 3–4
SECOND READING	2 Timothy 2:8–13
GOSPEL	Luke 17:11–19

✺ Naaman the leper obeys the command of Elisha the prophet and is made whole. He returns praising the God of Israel as the only God and declares that he is now the servant now of this God. Elisha will not take his gift—the power was God's alone and instead he takes earth from the land of Israel, where God is Lord. Paul is writing Timothy from prison and reminding him that his sufferings are bound to other believers' needs. We who have died with Christ (in baptism and persecution) will also rise with him but we must hold on and be faithful. We must be sure not to deny God when times are hard or we grow tired.

Jesus is met by ten lepers, one of them a Samaritan and they beg him for healing. He heals them all and they return, seeking acceptance from the temple so that they may pick up their lives again. And only one returns to bless God in Jesus—the Samaritan. Jesus tells him to stand up (resurrection life) and to go his way for now he knows faith and salvation and not just respite from his illness. All of us have been forgiven, strengthened, healed repeatedly—do we live lives of thanksgiving (eucharist) by sharing all we have with others in gratitude? Does our liturgy get expressed in our lives or do we use God for what we want/need and then forget all about who God is and what God has done for us?

A   TWENTY-NINTH SUNDAY IN ORDINARY TIME

FIRST READING   Isaiah 45:1, 4–6
Responsorial Psalm   Psalm 96:1, 3, 4–5, 7–8, 9–10
SECOND READING   1 Thessalonians 1:1–5b
GOSPEL   Matthew 22:15–21

The Pharisees and their hated enemies, the Herodians together take counsel on how to trap Jesus in his own words. First they try to set him up with flattery and then drive home the question they think will trip him up: "is it against the Law to pay taxes to Caesar or not?" If he answers no then the Herodians can accuse him of treason and if he says yes than the Pharisees can use that against him with the people. But Jesus is angered. He asks for a coin (which according to the Law of God, they should not have had in their possession because of the image on it—Caesar who claimed to be god and the coin bore the inscription: Caesar is god.) Jesus is a rabbi and he knows the heritage of the Jewish religion. He asks whose image is on the coin—knowing the echo of those words (whose image are we made in—God's alone). There was a debate earlier that all the Pharisees and others would be aware of—that when a ruler makes coins with his image they are uniform, all the same, but when God makes human beings in his image, no one is like another and each reveals the glory of God. Jesus refuses to be caught in their trap and instead calls them to remember whom they belong to—GOD ALONE. And once you admit honestly to that, then it changes all other choices. They however, do not believe and they have been caught at their own dishonesty and collusion with those who have occupied their country and oppressed them for decades. They do not give God what is due God.

B   TWENTY-NINTH SUNDAY IN
ORDINARY TIME

FIRST READING   Isaiah 53:10–11
Responsorial Psalm   Psalm 33:4–5, 18–19, 20, 22
SECOND READING   Hebrews 4:14–16
GOSPEL   Mark 10:35–45 (or Mark 10:42–45)

☀ The just servant suffers yet is blessed with life, with light and knowledge. What is suffered saves others. Jesus is priest, yet one who has suffered and remained faithful so we are called to accept our sufferings and live justly, approaching God with Jesus, knowing grace and mercy will be given to us. James and John (and most of us) are looking for places of power yet Jesus is asking them to closely follow him on the way of the cross to the glory of resurrection life. Our baptisms/confirmation and eucharist invite us always into the suffering, death and resurrection of Jesus. Do we accept his offer?

C   TWENTY-NINTH SUNDAY IN
ORDINARY TIME

FIRST READING   Exodus 17:8–13
Responsorial Psalm   Psalm 121:1–2, 3–4, 5–6, 7–8
SECOND READING   2 Timothy 3:14—4:2
GOSPEL   Luke 18:1–8

☀ Amalek wages war against the Israelites. Joshua is the leader in the battle while Moses stands on a high place and lifts his staff high. As long as his arms are raised the Israelites are winning and when he weakens, they begin to weaken. Aaron and Hur help hold up his arms so that the Israelites can finally conquer their enemies. What if this image of prayer was used, not to wage war, but to stop it now—as Jesus' followers are never to harm or kill another as they practice loving one another as God has loved us in Jesus. We must read the Scriptures with faith—through the eyes of God in Jesus and use it as reproof, correction and training in holiness—not to shore up our own convictions or to make points against another. This is our work, the work of God entrusted to us—to make the world holy.

We are to pray always and not lose heart. There is nothing that cannot be brought about by prayer: a world with no war, a world with justice and reconciliation, where all peoples' needs for survival and life taken care of, a world where there is no hatred and animosity, no matter how diverse we are. But we must learn that we are not so much like the widow (who is God) but we are much more like the unjust judge and that God is intent on calling us to justice and conversion. But will we ever learn? When our God comes, will he find any faith among those who claim to be his own?

A THIRTIETH SUNDAY IN ORDINARY TIME

FIRST READING   Exodus 22:20–26
Responsorial Psalm   Psalm 18:2-3, 3–4, 47, 51
SECOND READING   1 Thessalonians 1:5c–10
GOSPEL   Matthew 22:34–40

The year grows short and the questions more direct. Once again they are going at Jesus. He has just silenced the stupid arguments of the Sadducees who did not believe in resurrection or judgment. Now the Pharisees will have another go at Jesus and one approaches with the age-old Jewish question: "Which is the most important commandment in the Law?" Jesus answers with the Shema—which is both a prayer to the holiness of God and the foundational call to the covenant and basis of all the law—to love God with all your mind, heart, soul and resources. But Jesus adds in, the second (like both sides of your hand) to love your neighbor with the same passion and wholeheartedness. Everything in the law, the prophets, the history of faithfulness in the Jewish covenant is based on putting these words into practice and obeying the intent of God that all who are made in his image, live in his image as truthfully as we can. And there is no getting around it—no hedging, no rationalizing. And we—who are we like: the Sadducees playing games with theology; the Pharisees and those using the law to test, trick and make others stumble—or are we with Jesus, intent on the worship of God and the care of human beings?

B THIRTIETH SUNDAY IN ORDINARY TIME

FIRST READING — Jeremiah 31:7–9
Responsorial Psalm — Psalm 126:1–2, 2–3, 4–5, 6
SECOND READING — Hebrews 5:1–6
GOSPEL — Mark 10:46–52

We are called to rejoice, and shout out the praise of God for all nations to hear, even though we are a remnant of God's people returning home. And we are a motley crew: lame, blind, mothers, women in labor, weeping, coming from everywhere, led to waters of life. Our God and priest is from among us, knowing weakness with us, bound to us and offering sacrifices with us and for us, as beloved children of Our Father/God. Are we careful of those among us that are blind, yet hearing the Word, seeking Jesus? Or are we like the disciples seeking to keep others quiet, keeping Jesus to ourselves? Bartimaeus begins to follow Jesus up the road, the way of the Cross—have we begun that journey or are we still busy keeping others away from Jesus, or still caught begging?

C THIRTIETH SUNDAY IN ORDINARY TIME

FIRST READING — Sirach 35:12–14, 16–18
Responsorial Psalm — Psalm 34:2–3, 17–18, 19, 23
SECOND READING — 2 Timothy 4:6–8, 16–18
GOSPEL — Luke 18:9–14

Our God is the God of justice. God hears the cry of the oppressed and is not deaf to the wail of the orphan or widow. The prayer of the lowly pierces the clouds—do we hear like God hears or are we deaf to others? God will affirm those who do what is right—does God have cause to affirm us? Paul is in prison and is looking at death approaching him. He prays that God the judge will award him and all those who have looked forward to his coming. The Lord is with him, in court, in prison and always. Do we live with this faith and hope and rely on God's presence with us when it is hard to see how what is happening to us can be for our good?

Jesus tells us of the two who go to pray: one lists everything he does that is right and good—in case God hasn't noticed or appreciated what he has done for him, in obeying the law and being religious. And then there is the man who knows his sin and asks mercy—keeping his distance—crying out. The prayer of the man who knows who he is in truth before God is heard, long before the other who disdains others and does not know God or himself. How do we pray?

A   THIRTY-FIRST SUNDAY IN ORDINARY TIME

FIRST READING   Malachi 1:14b—2:2b, 8–10
Responsorial Psalm   Psalm 131:1, 2, 3
SECOND READING   1 Thessalonians 2:7b–9, 13
GOSPEL   Matthew 23:1–12

Jesus preaches openly to the people, warning them not to do what the leaders do, but to obey the word they speak. They don't obey their own teachings, laying burdens on the poorest, the widow and those struggling just to survive. They are intent on their own positions and honor, not God's. We must remember that we are all the brothers and sisters of Jesus, in one family and we call God, OUR FATHER and Christ is our only leader—the crucified one, beloved of God. We must imitate Jesus who humbled himself among us and we are to care for one another as Jesus has cared for us, revealing God's concern for us all. We must live truthfully with the honor of our calling as the beloved children of God and we must live humbly with the remembrance that it is our God who has loved us and brought us to live with one another in justice and peace. We must be careful that we do what we claim to believe in and not live lives that decry our words. The year is almost gone—if we were to be judged on this year and our lives' truthfulness what would our God have to say about us?

B   THIRTY-FIRST SUNDAY IN ORDINARY TIME

FIRST READING   Deuteronomy 6:2–6
Responsorial Psalm   Psalm 18:2–3, 3–4, 47, 51
SECOND READING   Hebrews 7:23–28
GOSPEL   Mark 12:28b–34

The year is drawing to a close and we are summoned to declare as a people where we stand before God. We are to fear God, listen and obey the commandments, with love that is all encompassing. We stand with Jesus our priest/leader so that we approach God, with Jesus interceding on our behalf. Jesus is our sacrifice that makes us holy before God, with him. How devotedly do we love God: with all our heart, soul, mind, resources, body and strength that endures? And do we love our neighbor/enemy/friend with the same passion? Then today, we will hear Jesus tell us that we are not far from the kingdom of God—God wants that practical love more than any sacrifice. God wants us as a people.

C THIRTY-FIRST SUNDAY IN ORDINARY TIME

FIRST READING   Wisdom 11:22—12:2
Responsorial Psalm   Psalm 145:1–2, 8–9, 10–11, 13, 14
SECOND READING   2 Thessalonians 1:11—2:2
GOSPEL   Luke 19:1–10

We are drawing to the end of the year 2007, and we must be mindful that we are always before the Lord in need of mercy, conscious of our sin and the effects our lives have on everyone else in the universe. God the Creator preserves and loves all that he has made. But often we who have been entrusted with it do not. We must ask forgiveness and seek to repair and bring forth God's Spirit that dwells in all things. When our God comes we must have a world and lives to give back to him that are filled with holiness.

The story of Zacchaeus who gives half of what he owns to the poor and does four fold restitution to anyone he has treated unjustly was the criteria for baptism in the early church and often was used as a model for all believers at the beginning of lent. And so it is fitting too that we look at this response to Jesus' invitation to share Eucharist with him and amend our lives accordingly. This late in the year, what do we owe in justice, in love, and in thanksgiving for all that God has shared with us?

A THIRTY-SECOND SUNDAY IN ORDINARY TIME

FIRST READING   Wisdom 6:12–16
Responsorial Psalm   Psalm 63:2, 3–4, 5–6, 7–8
SECOND READING   1 Thessalonians 4:13–18
GOSPEL   Matthew 25:1–13

The Pharisees try to accuse Jesus of encouraging his disciples to disobey the traditions of the elders of their religion. And Jesus in anger theologizes and carefully and surely separates out the law of God from mere traditions that can be used to escape from the responsibility of obeying the law. He uses the example of those who in publicly devoting themselves to religion, do not care for their parents. He calls them hypocrites, who do not worship God and only deal with human rules. Then he teaches what is truthful and pure and what is not—that what a person does or says is what defiles a person not what they eat or how they ate. The Pharisees are offended and Jesus is more offended—declaring that what is not planted by God will be uprooted. Are our actions and works planted in the Word and kingdom of God among those who need them or are we about looking good to others and deciding on what we will do, according to our own convenience? Do people and God's will for life for those needing it come first? Jesus, plant your Word and Spirit deep in us and save us. Amen.

B THIRTY-SECOND SUNDAY IN ORDINARY TIME

FIRST READING   1 Kings 17:10–16
Responsorial Psalm   Psalm 146:7, 8–9, 9–10
SECOND READING   Hebrews 9:24–28
GOSPEL   Mark 12:38–44 (or Mark 12:41–44)

Elijah orders the widow of Zarephath to give him a drink and she obeys. Then he asks for a piece of bread, but she has none. She is preparing to die with her child. Yet her obedience, and care for a stranger gives her life. For years with the prophet, they live on the meal that does not run out.

We too live on the life and sacrifice of Jesus given once but endures and remains. The widow in the temple gives out of her sustenance, all that she has to live on, more than anything others give. And Jesus proclaims that she is like him, giving to God true sacrifice of life and self. What do we give our God?

C THIRTY-SECOND SUNDAY IN ORDINARY TIME

FIRST READING 2 Maccabees 7:1–2, 9–14
Responsorial Psalm Psalm 17:1, 5–6, 8, 15
SECOND READING 2 Thessalonians 2:16—3:5
GOSPEL Luke 20:27–38 (or Luke 20:27, 34–38)

We hear the gruesome story of the brutal killing of seven brothers and their mother forced to watch them suffer and die. But they all encourage each other to remain faithful and cling to the hope of resurrection and vindication for their integrity. How insignificant are some of our moments of choosing to be faithful to God's Word in comparison! And yet, we have been given the Spirit of God for consolation and also to strengthen us so that we might do justice, preach the gospel in our deeds and help others to progress in their obedience to the Gospel. What is the ground line of our lives is that God rules our hearts (where our will is) and that we live loving all others as God has loved us.

We stake our lives on the resurrection. We believe God the Father has raised Jesus from the dead in the power of the Spirit and that we too will be raised by the Father in the power of the Spirit. In fact, we live that resurrection life now in Christ through our baptisms. We do not know what that life will be like but we believe that it will be the fullness of life, as the children of God with Jesus. We live now, our lives given over in sacrifice (made holy) to our God who is the God of the living. We must keep this in mind now—so that when we die, we can reach for this hope with confidence.

A THIRTY-THIRD SUNDAY IN ORDINARY TIME

FIRST READING Proverbs 31:10–13, 19–20, 30–31
Responsorial Psalm Psalm 128:1–2, 3, 4–5
SECOND READING 1 Thessalonians 5:1–6
GOSPEL Matthew 25:14–30 (or Matthew 25:14–15, 19–21)

✹ The parable of the talents (silver) and someone giving money to invest before they go away. Each is given according to their perceived ability. The first two do well and double their investment; the last digs a hole for safe keeping. Upon his return, it's judgment. The first two are rewarded as good and faithful servants and share their master's joy. The last describes his master as hard, and basically a thief!! And the master is furious and takes his talent (money) and gives it to the one who made the most profit for the master. "To those who have, more will be given, and they will have an abundance; but from those who are unproductive, even what they have will be taken from them." And the useless servant is thrown out into the dark. Harsh parable. What if the ruthless master is not God but Jesus is describing how the world works? Because the very next line reads…when the Son of Man comes …and it is the judgment of the sheep and the goats—the way God in Jesus will judge. Do we live our lives like those in the world or following our Master who is not like those of the world?

B THIRTY-THIRD SUNDAY IN ORDINARY TIME

FIRST READING — Daniel 12:1–3
Responsorial Psalm — Psalm 16:5, 8, 9–10, 11
SECOND READING — Hebrews 10:11–14, 18
GOSPEL — Mark 13:24–32

✹ The visions of Daniel are of endings/anguish and salvation for the faithful ones. Those who have the knowledge of God will shine forth like stars. There will be horrible things, abominable idols and irreligion but for us it suffices to remain true. And Jesus the sacrifice and priest is seated at the right hand of God in power, and one day all will know that power. The year is coming to an end and we are given sight of the end of all things, not to instill fear in us, but hope and courage! Our God, the Son of Man, Jesus crucified will come in judgment. We are to stand fast, together, no matter what happens on earth. Always, in all things, our God is with us.

C   THIRTY-THIRD SUNDAY IN ORDINARY TIME

FIRST READING	Malachi 3:19–20a
Responsorial Psalm	Psalm 98:5–6 , 7–8, 9
SECOND READING	2 Thessalonians 3:7—12
GOSPEL	Luke 21:5–19

If we fear the name of the Lord more than we fear any nation or power, if we fear to dishonor God or disobey him, then the day is coming when we will see the sun of justice arise with its healing rays. But if we are proud and do evil then it will be our end. We are to live and imitate Jesus and those who followed him, even unto death. (some thought that the end was near and so they did not work—this does not refer to the poor, the sick, the ill, the infirm and the children, etc.) All the readings are about the end times—the end of this year, the end of Israel and the destruction of the temple, the end of any nation/power/empire's reign on the earth and one day, the end of the world. Jesus is clear—do not get caught up in this endtime craziness. There are going to be earthquakes, plagues, famines and war (there have been for 2000 years and probably many more thousands of years). Before it happens those who believe in Jesus will be persecuted, put on trial with the rulers of the world and killed. Most Christians are definitely not in this situation today—we are often the ones doing the killing and manhandling of other countries and peoples. We are to live now with the Spirit's inspiration, without violence or acting like the nations of the world. For us, let us look to this year's end and whether or not we have anything to give to God today.

A   OUR LORD JESUS CHRIST THE KING

FIRST READING	Ezekiel 34:11–12, 15–17
Responsorial Psalm	Psalm 23:1–2, 2–3, 5, 6
SECOND READING	1 Corinthians 15:20–26, 28
GOSPEL	Matthew 25:31–46

Our King is a Good Shepherd who cares for his own sheep leading them to pastures and protecting them from destruction. And he is judge of the nations, the Son of Man with all the power and glory of God. This is the last Sunday of Ordinary Time, of the year 2005. It is Judgment Day. Will we as a nation find ourselves with the sheep or with the goats? Is our nation known for compassion, care for the poor, providing the basic necessities of life—the demands of justice: food, water, clothing, shelter, medicine and freedom from oppression? Did this year belong to God? Did we serve our God and one another this year or are we in need of repentance and turning? O Jesus do not let us wander from you. Bring us back and save us.

B   OUR LORD JESUS CHRIST THE KING

FIRST READING   Daniel 7:13–14
Responsorial Psalm   Psalm 93:1, 1–2, 5
SECOND READING   Revelation 1:5–8
GOSPEL   John 18:33b–37

We stand in the presence of the One that Daniel saw in a vision: the Son of Man, facing the One of the Ages and all power is his, and every people, nation and language serve him. The kingdom will come in its fullness. Our God comes: Alpha and Omega, Jesus, firstborn from the dead who has washed us in his blood and presented us to God/Father. He comes with peace and grace forever! Our God Jesus, the King stands before Pilate, before the powers of this world and declares that he was born to bear witness to the truth and that anyone who hears his voice is on the side of truth. Where do we stand? Do we stand with the Son of Man, crucified in this world, with the truth of the Gospel? If we do not stand with him here, we will not stand with him forever in glory. Choose.

C   OUR LORD JESUS CHRIST THE KING

FIRST READING   2 Samuel 5:1–3
Responsorial Psalm   Psalm 122:1–2, 3–4, 4–5
SECOND READING   Colossians 1:12–20
GOSPEL   Luke 23:35–43

This is the last Sunday of the year of the Lord. Time for us to look at the year and its history of faithfulness or lack of it. We are to look at it in light of forever and hand it over to God as we hand over our lives as sacrifice/gift. Our King, our God, is a shepherd that gathers and holds us together in the face of what happens in the world. And our king is the image of the invisible God who has made us saints who live in the light. All things, in heaven, on earth and in the past, are under this power and command. Our king is the one who reconciles and makes whole again, makes holy. Our king is the crucified one, who would not kill, or lie, or live dishonestly in collusion with the powers of the world: political, nationalistic, economic or religious. He is the king who only loves God and all that God has created. And God's kingdom, or better called "kin-dom" is shared with those who need it the most, those who are rejects of the kingdoms of the world and those who recognize and accept the forgiveness and reconciling power of God in Jesus. This is the reality of history, of the universe, of daily and personal life no matter what those who rule in the world might say. Today we look at this year and see if it truly was the year of the Lord and if we have much to give back to our king crucified or do we need to cry out for the mercy of God and pray: "Lord, remember me when you come into your glory and your reign."

SOLEMNITIES OF THE LORD DURING ORDINARY TIME

A   THE MOST HOLY TRINITY

FIRST READING   Exodus 34:4b–6, 8–9
Responsorial Psalm   Daniel 3:52, 53, 54, 55, 56
SECOND READING   2 Corinthians 13:11–13
GOSPEL   John 3:16–18

This is perhaps the most famous line of scripture: "God so loved the world that he gave his only Son that whoever believes in him may not be lost, but may have eternal life." But what exactly does it mean? All the words of Jesus in John's gospel speak of his primary love and relationship to the Father who has sent him, and that he does only what the Father desires and that the Father loves him because he obeys him and saves us. To save is to rescue from death and danger and Jesus' presence in the world, the Incarnation does just that. Jesus' words, works, healing, forgiving, love and association with the least of the earth, the despised of the world confronts history and power and alters all the future. Our God is life and love, mercy and justice and without violence, rancor, or destruction. But we are judged, and either saved or condemned by whether or not we take to heart the presence of God among us and love God in one another. The mystery of the Trinity tells us that our God is community: Father, Son who is Lord of all the earth and Spirit binding us together. We must live in unity if we believe in God.

B   THE MOST HOLY TRINITY

FIRST READING   Deuteronomy 4:32–34, 39–40
Responsorial Psalm   Psalm 33:4–5, 6, 9, 18–19, 20, 22
SECOND READING   Romans 8:14–17
GOSPEL   Matthew 28:16–20

We have heard the voice of God (not at Sinai) but in Jesus, in the Word/Scriptures in community and we belong to God more closely even than Israel and we must be faithful in obeying our God's commandments together so that we proclaim God to all. In Jesus we are given the Spirit to call God Father. In baptism we are given the same relationship with the Father that Jesus has, with the power of the Spirit. We are drawn into the Trinity, the mystery of communion/community in God. And then we are to spend our lives living out that Trinity with all others in the world. A daunting task filled with grace and power.

C   THE MOST HOLY TRINITY

FIRST READING   Proverbs 8:22–31
Responsorial Psalm   Psalm 8:4–5, 6–7, 8–9
SECOND READING   Romans 5:1–5
GOSPEL   John 16:12–15

Wisdom has dwelled with God from the beginning even before creation, one with God as the earth and all that was made, playing before Him and being his delight and delighting to be with human beings. Wisdom has been a name for Jesus and for the Spirit. Do we love wisdom and seek the wisdom of the Word and the Spirit—we are at peace with God in Jesus and the love of God has been poured into our hearts by the Spirit, a gift given to us who believe.

Jesus seeks to tell us so much (knowledge from God's point of view) but we can't bear it. But the Spirit has been given to be our teacher, our companion, advocate, paraclete and comfort. All that the Father has given to Jesus the Spirit wishes to share with us and bring us to the fullness of truth. The wisdom that Jesus in the power of the Spirit wishes to share with us is the Father and brings us into the Trinity to be one with God—all that God has made to be in communion. We are invited to know this wisdom.

A   THE MOST HOLY BODY AND
BLOOD OF CHRIST

FIRST READING   Deuteronomy 8:2–3, 14b–16a
Responsorial Psalm   Psalm 147:12–13, 14–15, 19–20
SECOND READING   1 Corinthians 10:16–17
GOSPEL   John 6:51–58

✳ This is the mystery of the Body and Blood of Christ, of Eucharist in liturgy—the work of the people. But it is also the mystery of Jesus' teaching, of the Word made flesh that dwells among us in the Scriptures. We feast on the word, chew on it and swallow it, internalizing it so that it becomes part of us. We stand on our words in the creed, and offer our bodies and lives to God with the bread and wine. And God transforms the bread and wine into the presence of the Risen Lord, the Body and Blood of Christ and transforms us into the Body and Blood of Christ, the Church in the world, as food and justice, hope and peace for all. We eat what we have proclaimed and become what we eat, becoming God's presence in the world for it is life and salvation. We eat the Bread and the Word and we will live forever, even here, we will taste everlasting life in God, our Father, Jesus the Risen Lord, and the Spirit who binds us together.

B   THE MOST HOLY BODY AND BLOOD OF CHRIST

FIRST READING   Exodus 24:3–8
Responsorial Psalm   Psalm 116:12–13, 15–16, 17–18
SECOND READING   Hebrews 9:11–15
GOSPEL   Mark 14:12–16, 22–26

✳ We are bound in a covenant of flesh and blood. The people of Israel proclaimed publicly that they would obey the word of God and Moses sprinkles both the offerings to God and the people (who belong to God and are the real offerings) with the blood of the sacrifice. The blood binds them together in the book and the sacrifice. This is a faint image of the covenant of Jesus' word in flesh and blood and sacrifice that binds us forever to God and to one another in Word/Scripture and bread and wine, the flesh and blood of Jesus, the Body of Christ the Crucified and Risen Lord. This is the mystery of our binding to God the Father in Jesus in the power of the Spirit. Here we dwell with God and once we eat and drink we are to be that covenant together in the world.

C   THE MOST HOLY BODY AND BLOOD OF CHRIST

FIRST READING　　　　　　　　　Genesis 14:18–20
Responsorial Psalm　　　　　　Psalm 110:1, 2, 3, 4
SECOND READING　　　　　1 Corinthians 11:23–26
GOSPEL　　　　　　　　　　　　　　Luke 9:11b–17

The images of an offering/gift of bread consecrated to the Holy is ancient, as in the priest of Salem (not a Jew) Melchizedek, who blessed Abram in the name of the creator. But our sacrifice (what is made holy by giving to the service of God) is that of Jesus himself. It is not just what he did, but who he is—bread/wine—that we give. Our lives are made one with the body and blood of Jesus and we become one body, one spirit, one heart and mind with Jesus, the Body of Christ. This is what has been handed on to us from those who have believed and lived and died with Christ since the beginning. We 'do this'—eucharist/liturgy—and we are brought together in communion with God and one another. The ritual of eucharist must be expressed daily in the feeding of the world—bread, justice, peace, forgiveness—all that God has shared with us in Jesus, or else our worship of the Body of Christ remains empty and self-serving/self-righteous. Are we the Body of Christ in the world today—being the bread and the hope of those most in need?

A   SACRED HEART OF JESUS

FIRST READING　　　　　　　　　Deuteronomy 7:6–11
Responsorial Psalm　　　Psalm 103:1–2, 3–4, 6–7, 8, 10
SECOND READING　　　　　　　　　1 John 4:7–16
GOSPEL　　　　　　　　　　　　　　Matthew 11:25–30

This is one of Jesus' prayers to his beloved God-Father, out loud so that we are allowed to overhear and learn how close Jesus is with his God. Jesus praises God for his wisdom in teaching the poor and the simple, the non-violent the holiness of God. And he lets us know that everything has been entrusted to him by the Father and no one knows the Father except him and anyone he chooses to teach, and no one knows the Son except the Father. There is intimacy here, and secrecy and sanctuary. And then we are invited in, when we are weary from the work of the kingdom of justice and peace; invited to pick up the yoke of hard work, of suffering on the cross and the joy of community; and we are invited to learn of Jesus' inmost heart: that is gentle, non-violent (meek) and humble. Only here in Jesus' heart will we find rest, security, sanctuary and the strength to bear our share of the burden of the Gospel and our cross and learn the courage to ease others' burdens as God eases ours. This is a glimpse into Jesus' heart. It is a world that we are reluctant really to enter for it draws us deep into the mystery of suffering for others and love unto death, laying down our lives for one another with Jesus. Come!

B   SACRED HEART OF JESUS

FIRST READING   Hos 11:1, 3–4, 8c–9
Responsorial Psalm   Is 12:2–3, 4, 5–6
SECOND READING   Eph 3:8–12, 14–19
GOSPEL   John 19:31–37

In the days after Pentecost we celebrate deep mysteries of our God that are to sustain us all through ordinary time. Today we look at the love of God for us in Jesus' Spirit and Body. It has been there since the beginning but we are slow to see, understand and accept it. We are children held in arms, taught to walk, held in human cords, bands of love like an infant held to a cheek in tenderness. God is overwhelmed with love for us and so gives us Jesus, the Holy One always present among us, love burning yet not consuming us. It is love given in life and in death and in resurrection life—no end to its depth, breadth. We dwell in the heart of our God, with Jesus crucified, risen and sent in his Spirit. We live in the Trinity.

C SACRED HEART OF JESUS

FIRST READING   Ezk 34:11–16
Responsorial Psalm   Ps 23:1–3a, 3b–4, 5, 6
SECOND READING   Rom 5:5b–11
GOSPEL   Lk 15:3–7

❋ Jesus is the Shepherd that tends the sheep, rescuing them, gathering them together, leading them home, pasturing them, protecting them and giving them rest/peace. He seeks out the lost, forgiving, bringing back the strays, binding the injured, but destroying the sleek and the strong—shepherding all with justice. This is the love of the heart of God in Jesus.

This love has been shared with us in the life/death/resurrection of Jesus. God is not/has not ever been wrathful even when we have been inhuman. All we have known is God's reconciliation and mercy in Jesus the Lord. We have each been the one, lost and straying that has been brought back to the other sheep—so that we could all be one again in God. The Shepherd wants to keep us all together. The heart of Jesus seeks to bring us all into the fullness of God, the Trinity so that we might dwell as one.

FEASTS OF THE LORD
AND SAINTS

February 2

THE PRESENTATION OF THE LORD

FIRST READING — Malachi 3:1–4
Responsorial Psalm — Psalm 24:7, 8, 9, 10
SECOND READING — Hebrews 2:14–18
GOSPEL — Lk 2:22–40

Traditionally this is the last day of the Epiphany season when Jesus, the first born of Joseph and Mary is ritually given in obedience to the service of Yahweh, the God of the people Israel in thanksgiving for their release from bondage in Egypt. It is a feast of Light, when the Light of God begins to move into the world of ordinary time and history, growing surely and truthfully in the power of the Spirit of God in the person of Jesus. The family is met by Simeon the old faithful prophet silent in waiting on the time of God and he cries out in joy and hope that is present. This is "the light [God is] revealing to the nations" and God has let him see it in his lifetime, graciously. There will be resistance, and those closest to the Light will know their own hearts torn open, exposed and sorrowful because of closeness to the burning fire of God. The ritual finished, the child grows in wisdom; God's grace upon him. This is our way of salvation: we have seen the Light in the Word made flesh. Now we are to grow in wisdom through obedience and bring that Light into the world in our flesh and lives.

The prophet cries out that the one awaited will enter the sanctuary and is already here. Can we bear his presence, a refiner's fire that makes pure silver and gold ? And Jesus is brought into the temple and presented to the Lord in accordance with the law of Moses. First born he belongs to God alone. He will be peace. He will be a sign of contradiction in Israel. He will be the prophet who is the Word of the Lord. He is subject to human beings and to the Word of God. We too are presented to God in our baptism. Is this Word of God refining us into pure silver and gold, as Jesus was through obedience?

✣ The messenger went before the Lord, a refiner's fire, the fuller's lye, intent on purifying the children of God—this was as it was in the days gone by. But the one heralded has come and it is Jesus, who is like us in every way, but faithful and merciful before God on our behalf. Jesus was tempted, and suffered and so he can help us when we find ourselves in need.

Jesus was brought to the temple, in accordance with the law, to be given over—the first born to God on behalf of the people. And some of the remnant that waits in hopes are there and rejoice on seeing him. Simeon who blesses God, for now he can die in gratitude, crying out in joy, and declaring this child destined to be the cause of the rise and fall of many, a sign opposed and we, all of us will be pierced with the sword (of the Word of God) so that many will be laid bare. And Anna ever watchful blesses God and speaks of the child to those who look for deliverance. Are we waiting for the Word of God to be made manifest? Are we like the remnant Simeon, Anna, Joseph and Mary?

March 19

SAINT JOSEPH, HUSBAND
OF THE BLESSED VIRGN MARY

FIRST READING   2 Samuel 7:4–5a, 12–14a, 16
Responsorial Psalm   Psalm 89:2–3, 4–5, 27, 29
SECOND READING   Romans 4:13, 16–18, 22
GOSPEL   Matthew 1:16, 18–21, 24
                                 (or Luke 2:41–51a)

✣ Today is the feast of Joseph, the dreamer, the just man who obeys the Word of God, in scripture and dreams seeking the life of those around him. He is the man who adopted a son who was the beloved child of God, taking the woman Mary and her child into his heart and caring for them, giving them life and protection. He names Jesus—Joshua—savior of his people and it is from Joseph that Jesus learns to be a man, a Jew, a human being under oppression in occupied territory, yet obedient to the Law and to the prophets. Like David, his ancestor who sought to build a house for the Mighty God, Joseph does build a house, a sanctuary and dwelling place for God, Emmanuel God with us in the embrace and reach of his daily work and love. Lord, may we dream like Joseph and be as just, knowing how to interpret the Word of God to protect all in harm's way.

✹ Though having a lineage fit for royalty—being a descendant of David—we find Joseph to be a very humble man. He is a silent person, not given to many words, and yet he is a presence that inspires. It is this same presence and humility that inspired Mary and Jesus himself. This stems from an energy that finds its source in God with whom Joseph had constant communication. And it doesn't end there, for Joseph listens and responds and trusts. Do we have that communication with God? Do we listen, respond and trust? Are we a presence that inspires?

✹ I will be a father to him and he shall be a son to me. These words of God to David can be rightly said of Joseph to Jesus and of God to Joseph. Jesus grew up in a Jewish family and Joseph would have taught him how to be a man, a Jew, a member of the people and of the covenant with God, faithful, obedient and prayerful. It was Joseph who taught him the law and the prophets, the rites and the customs of being Jewish, by example, and by word and as his teacher. Whatever Jesus learned of being human as a man and as a father, he learned from Joseph. Joseph's 'faith was credited to him as justice' as surely as was Abraham who was the father of nations.

Joseph is described as obedient to the law, upright and just. And yet he must choose whether to put Mary away quietly (break the marriage covenant and force her to leave and live on her own) or expose her to the law (humiliation and even death by stoning together with her unborn child). Yet Joseph is the image in Matthew's gospel of the new believer, the follower of Jesus, who knows the heart and spirit of the law, and so disobeys it. Instead he relies on the Word of the Scripture and obeys the heart of the law that makes him husband and father, adopting Jesus as his own child. There is so much we can learn from Joseph about being faithful, about compassion and obedience, about God as Father, just as Jesus learned.

ANNUNCIATION OF THE LORD

FIRST READING   Isaiah 7:10–14; 8:10
Responsorial Psalm   Psalm 40:7–8, 8–9, 10, 11
SECOND READING   Hebrews 10:4–10
GOSPEL   Luke 1:26–38

✹ This feast fell in Holy Week and so is Easter Week. This is the familiar prophecy of a young woman who will bear a child whose name will be Emmanuel, God is with us. And the story of Gabriel sent to the young woman Mary inviting her to obey the Word and will of God for the long promised salvation of her nation. She will give birth to a child, but the child is not hers—the child is God's, born of the power of the Spirit, born for the people and to bring hope and salvation into the world. Mary is the model for all believers and we too are invited to bring the Word of God into the world through our flesh, our words and lives. We too are called to be the handmaids of the Lord (as Moses, David, Isaiah and others were named) and we too must pray: "Let it be done to me as you have said." Let the Word of God take flesh in us, the Body of Christ and may we bring that Word into the world that waits and needs it so desperately today.

✹ In the midst of Lent we remember the reality of the Incarnation, the coming of the Word of God to humankind and to Mary. Our God is made flesh. Our God is Word made flesh dwelling among us. As we walk the way of the cross, all the way to death, and resurrection's glory, we walk with God, human with us. We follow our human merciful God in Jesus. As Mary conceived the Word in her womb by the power of the Holy Spirit when the Most High overshadowed her, so we read daily the Word of God so that the Most High might overshadow us and bring forth God in our flesh by the power of the Spirit. Then during the Paschal mystery we too will die and rise with the Word made flesh among us. We must remember.

✹ Ahaz will not choose to obey and wearies God and in return he is told that a sign will be given anyway. A virgin will be with child and bear a son and shall name him Immanuel. This is the tradition that was fulfilled in history after Ahaz and was appropriated to describe Mary and all believers who bring Immanuel into the world in our flesh and word and history. This is the day of the announcement of the Incarnation—of the coming of Emmanuel—God is with us—into the world, in the flesh of Mary, a young woman of Nazareth, nowhere and anywhere. The Word of the Lord comes and she is deeply disturbed and wonders what the greeting means—and what all of this Word will mean.

Mary said yes to the coming of the messiah. And Luke uses Mary as the image of all those who hear the proclamation of the Incarnation and are deeply disturbed but say Yes to baptism and to bearing the Word made flesh into their own bodies, lives and history. In the midst of Jesus' Emmanuel—God with us soon to be crucified we are called to listen to the Word of God and once again commit ourselves to believing, to obeying and to offering our bodies as sacrifice to the Lord. And say those words again: I am the handmaid of the Lord, let it be done to me as you have said."

June 24

BIRTH OF ST. JOHN THE BAPTIST

FIRST READING   Isaiah 49:1–6
Responsorial Psalm   Psalm 139:1–3, 13–14
SECOND READING   Acts 13:22–26
GOSPEL   Luke 1:57–66, 80

This is the child called from his mother's womb to be a prophet to the nations. He was formed to be a sharpened sword, a polished arrow held in Yahweh's hand until the time was fulfilled. And then he was let loose! John the prophet was sent to bring back the people to their God and to make the light shine forth as a signal to all the nations. This is the man child named John in obedience to the angel's word and in naming the child, his father's tongue is loosed and he praises God who is doing great things in Israel. This child goes before the Lord and prepares them for freedom, for forgiveness and mercy unknown before on earth. This man brings mercy to earth, light in the darkness, strong in the Spirit and then he appears in Israel openly preaching. What child is this? Once again we need to pray our God to send prophets, call them from the womb, to prepare God's way among us, to instill fear of the Lord once again in the people and to speak and live with the hand of God upon them.

❉ The city of Jerusalem is destroyed, the temple burned, the kings and their families executed and the people driven into exile, except for some of the poor who stay behind. The people turned from their covenant and God was with them, but He did not save them. The religion of Jesus is about living in the world, with its sufferings, illness, wars, politics and economics, and society. And yet lives an alternative of hope: healing, drawing those excluded in, welcoming and bringing life to all in circumstances of harm, misery, hunger and lack. It is not easy but it is the will of God for life for all. This is our life daily.

June 29

SAINTS PETER AND PAUL

FIRST READING	Acts 12:1–11
Responsorial Psalm	Psalm 34:2–3, 4–5, 6–7, 8–9
SECOND READING	1 Tim 4:6–8, 17–18
GOSPEL	Mt 16:13–19

❉ These are the towering figures of the early Church, yet both were very human men, with lacks and astounding graces. Peter speaks for the disciples when Jesus asks them: "Who do people say that I am?" and his answer is "Messiah, the Son of the Living God"—but that answer is given by the Father, and Peter does not understand the answer until after Jesus' death and resurrection and his own long conversion. This is the rock of the Church that was also a stumbling block, one who denied his Master, even cursing him. But he learned forgiveness and mercy at the hands of his Master and was made leader in the Church in the place of Jesus to go look for the lost sheep and care for the flock in unity. Paul, once persecuted and tortured Christians self-righteously, religiously and made the long journey to being a missionary and preacher, an apostle to the Gentiles, but he too was weak—and fell back on his Roman citizenship so that he would not suffer the humiliation and torture of crucifixion. Let us pray for leaders who learn forgiveness and mercy intent on the unity of the Church and also aware of the world and those who wait for the Good News in missionaries sent forth from the community.

✺ The history of the early church sees the death of James, and the imprisonment of Peter, and yet the church flourishes in the face of adversity and martyrdom, continuing the power of the crucified and risen Lord. After house-arrest, Paul too will die by being beheaded. They preached the Word and died for witnessing to Jesus. Jesus who is prophet, the Word of God made flesh among us, who is more than the awaited Messiah, the Son of God and Son of Man. And it is this Jesus who is with us and nothing in heaven or on earth, or even our own fighting will stand against the presence of the Body of Christ in the world.

✺ Peter is persecuted early and is detained in prison after the murder of James. The church prays for him and he is released mysteriously by the power of an angel saying: "Put on your belt and your sandals, and your cloak and follow me (see John 21). Peter will survive this time but one day he will be led to the cross. And Paul is in prison, writing to Timothy, waiting to die and speaking of what he has done by preaching to the nations. He is relying on God to bring him to the end.

Jesus demands that his disciples tell him who they think he is—others think he is a prophet (true enough—do we see Jesus as a prophet?) but he wants to push them further. It is Peter who answers that he is the Messiah, the Son of the Living God—knowledge that has been given to him by the Father, though it will take years and the experience of Jesus' death to give him understanding of what those words mean. Peter is bound to the foundation of the church with the promise that nothing will stand against it for Jesus will be with them, to forgive and to hold bound those who do evil. These first leaders were very human, and sinful, as we are—yet we need to call our leaders today to the cross and to the preaching of the gospel and hold those who do evil bound for their words/works.

ASSUMPTION OF THE BLESSED VIRGIN MARY

FIRST READING	Revelation 11:19; 12:1–6a, 10ab
Responsorial Psalm	Psalm 45:10, 11, 12, 16
SECOND READING	1 Corinthians 15:20–27
GOSPEL	Lk 1:39–56

✴ On this day we sing the song of Mary carrying Jesus, the Word of God made flesh among us. Called "The Magnificat"—it is the praise and glory of God, a litany of what God has done for his people from the beginning of time, remembering God's promises of life, and freedom. It is all about God and God's goodness to human beings and his goodness to Mary. And it is about the goodness that God will do for us in Jesus who is Life given to us: he will confuse the proud in their innermost hearts; he will depose the mighty and raise the lowly (without violence); and feed those who are hungry, and send the rich away empty. These are the mighty deeds of God upon the earth. This is the child of the Book of Revelation. This is the child, the shepherd of the nations. This is how salvation comes.

✴ We begin with John's vision while he is in exile. And the people he loves, his beloved community is under terrible persecution. His vision is one of struggle on a universal level between good and evil and of a woman giving birth to the one who saves. The woman is the church that is to give birth to the children of God as a woman gave birth to the Son of Man. It is both a symbolic telling of what God has done for us in Jesus Crucified and Risen and how that will come to fulfillment at the end of time for those born of God. We stake our lives on the resurrection of Jesus: that the Father has raised Jesus from the dead in the power of the Spirit and that God will do the same for us. There will be a time when we will know the fullness of life in God with Christ.

Mary is the mother of Jesus, but to be holy, she had to become a disciple of Jesus as everyone else is called—to believe in the Word of God, obey it with others in community and live in the power of the Spirit. Elizabeth confirms Mary's act of faith and the four of them: Elizabeth, John, Mary and Jesus—stand before God filled with the life of God coming into the world.

THE TRANSFIGURATION
OF THE LORD

FIRST READING	Daniel 7:9–10, 13–14
Responsorial Psalm	Psalm 97:1–2, 5–6, 9
SECOND READING	2 Peter 1:16–19
GOSPEL	**I.** Mt 17:1–9; Lk 9:28–36
	II. Mk 9:2–10

Six days later—the seventh day, after the call to the cross, Jesus takes his three closest friends up a mountain to pray and they are given a glimpse of the glory of God shining through him. He is transfigured: trans—across or through. Figure—the human body. The transfiguration is seeing through the body of Jesus or passing through and going across the body of Jesus into the presence of the living God. They see Moses and Elijah and think of Jesus in terms of great men of their tradition: lawgivers, liberators and prophets and are not listening to him and his words in their fear and so the Father commands them: LISTEN TO HIM, not to anyone else. There is no one else but Jesus. Who do we listen to—our own fears and insecurities, lost hopes, governments, groups, friends who do us harm, the societies of the world? We are to listen only to Jesus: to the Word of the Scriptures, to the poor, to the prophets. To listen means to obey. Do we?

The prophet Habakkuk cries out to God to see those who do wickedness and how they appear to flourish and rise, doing violence to the people of God. But God responds saying: "Write down the vision. Its time will come, wait for it. Those who do violence have no integrity but the just will live." This is the truth of the Word of God. Jesus is approached by a man begging for the life of his child who is demented and always trying to harm himself. Jesus heals the child, when his disciples cannot. They (and me) lack trust to face evil in the world. We are weak in faith and need to be converted as surely as the young child needs to be delivered from what harms him. Every generation must change.

Daniel has a vision of the Son of Man coming on the clouds of heaven and approaching the Ancient One—all in creation is given to him in honor, glory and dominion. The vision is one of power and awesomeness that defies anything on earth. This is Jesus the Son of Man coming in glory to judge the nations with justice. This is Jesus, the beloved child of God, declared by the Father at his baptism in the power of the Spirit. We are told to keep our attention (eyes, ears, heart, all of us) closely fixed on Jesus' prophetic Word as though we were watching a lamp shining in the darkest part of nigh. We wait for the morning star—Jesus crucified and risen from the dead to return in his glory—and in the meantime for this Jesus to rise in our own hearts. We are to rise, and not be afraid—there is only Jesus. Are we listening to this Word of God made flesh—is the Word, the prophetic word becoming flesh in us?

September 14

THE TRIUMPH OF THE
THE CROSS

FIRST READING   Nunmbers 21:4–9
Responsorial Psalm   Psalm 78:1–2, 34–35, 36–37, 38
SECOND READING   Philippians 2:6–11
GOSPEL   John 3:15–17

In the ancient Church this was the first day of Lent, the time of turning more intently into the following of Jesus and renewing the ardor of our first devotion to God at our baptisms. Like the people of the desert we speak out against God and are in need of acknowledging our sin, and interceding for one another. We must look upon Jesus the Crucified, without sin who draws us close to God in his person and presence among us. We belong to the Crucified One, humble and obedient, even unto death. Today we look and bend in worship and gratitude before the depth of the love of God for us...again.

The seraph was mounted on a pole and the people were told to look at it—to look at what had bitten them. And they were healed and recovered. This bronze serpent is seen as an image of Jesus on the Cross. But Jesus went to the cross, under the burden of people's hatred. He took it upon himself to live the way of God truthfully and to die clinging to God and being obedient to God's will, even if that meant being rejected and killed. Jesus was the fullness of God, God in our flesh and blood and he humbled himself to come and live with us as a human being, dying with us, even dying on a cross as the least of us. Somehow this mystery of the incarnation of God is what we are to become—we, our flesh and blood in Jesus are to become the Body of Christ given in love to the Father in the power of the Spirit. Our humanness is to become the holiness of God. This is our salvation. We are loved and given the very life of God in Jesus.

Does it feel like Lent? Monastic Lent began on this day and the liturgical calendar reflect this still. It is time to look upon our God, upon the cross and kiss the symbol of our life and recognize that we are made in the sign of the cross.

✴ In the early church and still among monastics today is the beginning of Lent! And so the readings call us to discipleship: to the way of the cross, to laying down our lives in service to one other, to love like God's for us, to be humble like Jesus the Lord who humbled himself unto death on a cross and saved us by forgiving and loving and believing in the goodness of his Father, faithful in the Spirit until the end. And so God raised him and we, who are saved in baptism/eucharist and life in the Body of Christ on the way to the cross and glory must honor him in word, in truth and with our own lives in obedience. This is our blessing, our heritage, our calling and responsibility—to love and to love as passionately and freely, everyone, as the Father loves the Son and the Spirit and they all love one another—we are invited into that love. Pick up the cross of glory and enter in!

November 1

ALL SAINTS DAY

FIRST READING	Revelation 7:2–4, 9–14
Responsorial Psalm	Psalm 24:1–2, 3–4, 5–6
SECOND READING	1 John 3:1–3
GOSPEL	Matthew 5:1–12

✴ We draw near to the end of ordinary time in the year of the Lord 2005 and we celebrate all the great servants of the Lord who will be sealed with the mark of God. They come from every race, nation, people and tongue on earth and they are clothed in white (baptism) and resurrection because they have been faithful in the face of trial and the world's history that persecutes and rejects and ignores the Word of God. These are the saints of God. We are the saints of God, called in our place and time to be holy. How? We are to practice poverty (sharing with others), mourn the sufferings of others, be gentle (non-violent), hunger and thirst for justice and holiness, be merciful to all, make peace on earth, be pure of heart, loving God first and all others in God and be willing to be persecuted, even killed for the preaching and bringing of Good News to the poor. When we do these things we are blessed even now and saved forever. God, make us saints today, servants marked with your sign of salvation: the cross. In the name of the Father, the Son and the Holy Spirit. Amen.

✴ We see/hear the vision of John, as God sends out his angels to bring into heaven all those sealed and saved, an impossible number to count, to stand before the throne of the Lamb of God/ Son of Man/Jesus. With the angels, they cry aloud victory to God and worship together. And some stand out: those who endured persecution, even being martyred and have robes washed in the blood of the Lamb. We are God's own children, (first in baptism and always, in God) and yet we do not sense what we will be! But we must purify ourselves so that we are as pure as Christ! We are the saints—one day to live in glory!

✴ John's vision in exile is one of hope and the gathering of the saints (those baptized who have sought to love God and live their baptismal vows) with the angels marking those saved. The saints come from everywhere—they are those who have followed the Lamb (who was sacrificed) and they too sought to give their lives to God daily in obedience and worship. Now they know the Lamb of God in glory and their baptismal garments are washed in the blood of the Lamb.

We are the children of God! Do we believe that and do we recognize one another as such? What we can be and will be cannot be imagined yet but we will be like God. We start practicing here by being the poor of the world or with them, mourning and comforting others, being the lowly (the non-violent) and seeking justice like it was water. They are the merciful and forgiving, the pure of heart and the peacemakers and those persecuted because they stand with all these people and stand faithful to God in the world that demands subservience to nations/powers. We are the saints, the children of God.

ALL SOULS DAY

FIRST READING   Wisdom 3:1–9
Responsorial Psalm   Psalm 23:1–3, 3–4, 5, 6
SECOND READING   Romans 6:3–9
GOSPEL   Matthew 25:31–46

There will be a day when there are no more tears or suffering and death will be no more. A feast will be prepared for all peoples and our God will be so close as to wipe our tears away. But we must be among those who waited for the Lord to save us and rejoiced in his Word, then we will rest with the hand of Yahweh upon us. Jesus calls us not to the feasts of this world, but the wedding feast of the Lamb, the banquet of heaven where life is shared with all. All are invited here but so many of us make excuses: family, business, greed, another sale, expansion of profit and so those crippled, make lame, the blind and the poor will be brought in before us and many invited will not truly eat of the feast of God. Jesus, we pray for those who have gone before us—may they know the feast and one day, may we too sit at table with you and those we have long loved, and all the friends of God in your kingdom. Amen.

We are told of the promise that awaits those who are faithful, who endure and are just on earth. We will shine like sparks that ignite stubble and they will penetrate the truth, knowing God's mercy and grace in God's embrace. Christ lived and died and is alive again, living and dying for us and with us that we might be reconciled and live in God, now and forever. Jesus prays to the Father, letting us have a glimpse of how he lives in God, and how we can live in God with him and the Spirit, even now. Let us pray that this wisdom will be shared with us, and we will be yoked to one another and God here and hereafter.

Our souls live in hope and we believe that one day we will shine like sparks that run in the stubble and that it is the just who will one day govern and rule. And more importantly, if we trust in God we will penetrate the truth and live with God in love because of his mercy. We have been baptized into the dying and rising of Jesus and our resurrections have begun. Our lives are practice for the fullness of glory with God. This is the foundation of our religion and all our lives' practice and prayer. We will all die, but we stake our lives on the hope that the Son of Man will come in glory to judge each person and all the nations and that there will be life everlasting. And today we pray for all those who have gone before us in faith. And we pray that they who know more than we do now of God's presence will remember us before God too.

November 9

THE DEDICATION OF THE LATERAN BASILICA

FIRST READING	Ezekiel 47:1–2, 8–9, 12
Responsorial Psalm	Psalm 46:3, 4, 5–6, 8, 11
SECOND READING	1 Corinthians 3:9c–11, 16–17
GOSPEL	John 2:13–22

So early in the gospel of John Jesus moves radically to cleanse the temple in Jerusalem of its collusion in the economic and political system of the Roman Empire. He is described after forcefully evicting the merchants and money-changers as acting with 'zeal for the House of God that devours him as a fire.' Jesus is laying bare the shallowness of worship that is not based in self-sacrifice—the handing over of one's body, soul, mind and resources to God and the will and law of God, in service to the care of others and the coming of justice and peace. The new temple will be the Body of Christ, the Church—not the building but the people baptized into the Corpus Christi. When we worship in a church, we go forth to kneel and serve the broken Body of the Crucified in our world. Are we in need of cleansing?.

✣ We celebrate a mother church in Rome, a sanctuary made holy by long devotion and the gathering of those who believed, who practiced their faith and many who died in that witness to belief. Church is the place that we 'go forth from' (Martin Luther King, Jr) into the world with the waters of life, the tree of healing and food for body and soul. In reality, it is we who are the building, the Body of Christ, the Church in the world, the foundation of hope and liberation that others are seeking. It is up to us to share the Spirit within us concretely with others, with zeal, with passion and grace, generously. This is the worship of heart that God desires from us, as he received it from Jesus.

✣ Water flows from the temple and this water purifies and brings life to everything in its path and all that dwell in it, and drink from it. This water of the Spirit of life produces fruit every month and the food is good for eating and healing. This church is one of the oldest in Rome—a symbol for mother churches everywhere that plants, waters, gives life to all who are baptized/fed/forgiven and worship together in its confines/spaces. We are the Church and we build the foundation, not of buildings, but of relationships and freedom, justice and hope for all the peoples of the world. Church is the place that we go forth from and into the world for in service of others. We are to be much more careful of the temples of God—the people around us—than we are for the physical building structure. What we do in the building is nothing if we are not attentive to the needs of people and what we do for one another, as well as what our God has done for us, and what we would do in gratitude. It is time to rededicate ourselves to the building of the human community.

December 8

THE IMMACULATE CONCEPTION
OF THE BLESSED VIRGIN MARY

FIRST READING	Genesis 3:9–15, 20
Responsorial Psalm	Psalm 98:1, 2–3, 3–4
SECOND READING	Ephesians 1:3–6, 11–12
GOSPEL	Luke 1:26–38

✷ What have we done? Each of us was conceived in the 'eye' of God as some folk say and dreamed into flesh and blood. We were conceived by our God with an 'original face' of holiness and freedom and in Jesus we were chosen and blessed before the creation of the world to be holy and without sin in his presence. We were conceived in love to be the children of God, the brothers and sisters of Jesus. The woman Mary was conceived in this way and as a believer said "I am the handmaid of the Lord, let it be done to me as you have said." Like otwher handmaids before her, Moses, David, Isaiah and her son Jesus her word is given along with her body and her life to the blessing and praise of God and obedience to the will of God. What did God conceive us to be? Pray with Mary to submit to the Word made flesh among us and live in the freedom of God's children.

✷ The visions are elaborate, detailed, and symbolic: evil will be destroyed. The dead will be raised, judged before life; the old earth will pass away; there will be second deaths of judgment and there will be a new heaven and a new earth. What will they be like? We only know that holiness will prevail and it will be born of God. Is it close? Jesus says to look at the fig tree, every tree—watch the signs. Is God near? God is always near and every year there is judgment and newness of life. One day there will be ultimate justice and redemption. But for this year, do we belong to God?

✷ We hear one of the stories of our genesis—our first parents who symbolize all people created in the image and likeness of God, called to obey the Word of God. They failed—missed the mark and find themselves searching for knowledge of themselves, of God and knowing the freedom to do both good and evil. All of us struggle to know and obey God, since the beginning. Adam and Eve is each and everyone of us seeking and failing to know life in God. We have been recreated in baptism, sharing the life of God in Jesus and blessed beyond description. We are filled with the love of God. This is the will and pleasure of God—to make us all holy, to know God intimately and to live our lives in praise of God's goodness to us.

We hear the story of the beginnings of the incarnation and God sending his angel to declare God's presence that will be among us forever and all ways in a child born of a woman and the power of the Spirit of God, overshadowed by God (the Father). This is the account of the Trinity and the Incarnation, two core mysteries at the heart of our belief and practice. It is about Mary saying yes, her baptism and our saying yes so that God can be born, seeded into our souls, hearts and bodies.

ALSO AVAILABLE BY MEGAN MCKENNA

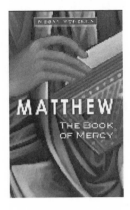

Matthew

The Book of Mercy

"Written for a popular audience, this commentary on Matthew's gospel ... underscores the evangelist's focus on mercy and forgiveness. Drawing on solid scholarship on Matthew, McKenna notes that Matthew's community lived at a time of tense transition in the early church.... Into her exposition of the text McKenna characteristically weaves stories from both Jewish and other cultural traditions. Reflection questions and suggestions for further study enhance the volume's usefulness for individual spiritual reading or group discussion."

Donald Senior, C.P.
The Bible Today

ISBN 978-1-56548-279-1
224 pp., paperback

Luke

The Book of Blessings and Woes

"McKenna explores the contemporary significance of the beatitudes and woes in Luke's sermon on the plain.... Her book is full of practical insight. It will be of most interest to those who seek to integrate their scholarly exegesis with practical application in ecclesial contexts."

Religious Studies Review

ISBN 978-1-56548-316-3
240 pp., paperback

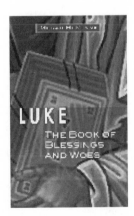

We Live Inside a Story

In the realm of the Spirit, and when dealing with our own souls and the souls of others, we are often at a loss for words. We have a sense, maybe even an image of what we want to share, ask, or communicate, but words are harder to find and express. Stories are the glue that hold us together in whatever groups we belong to, even if we only visit or find ourselves on the margins. In a sense, our God is a story being told and God is seeking for all of us to listen, to enter into the story and become one. Megan McKenna uses images of Russian nesting dolls to illustrate the many layers of the stories that exist in each of our lives, particularly in relation to the Spirit. Stories are critical to living and are intertwined with truth in such a way that we can carry them with us, remember them and pass them along, sharing them as needed. We live inside a story. We live inside God.

ISBN 978-1-56548-334-7
230 pp., paperback

The Hour of the Tiger
Facing Our Fears

It is about facing life and death, fear and love; about facing all the hard issues of life and all the mysterious, deep places of living. Megan McKenna has embraced the image of the tiger and chosen it to represent those of us who face our fears head on, or to highlight those of us who turn with the pack and run. Through stories, anecdotes and scriptural passages, the author encourages us to be not afraid, to take courage and grace in the living of life to its fullest, to lessen the encroachment of fear by knowing and recognizing the possibilities and experiences yet to be embraced.

ISBN 978-1-56548-325-5
184 pp., paperback

Advent, Christmas, Epiphany

Stories and Reflections on the Daily Readings

The lectionary readings for the entire Christmas season come alive through the stories and reflections of popular author Megan McKenna. Her words show us how we can center our lives on bringing justice and peace into the world while we wait for Jesus, the Son of God, to come among us. This volume includes readings for each day of the week.

978-1-56548-301-9
256 pp., paperback

Advent, Christmas, Epiphany

Stories and Reflections on the Sunday Readings

The lectionary readings for the entire Christmas season come alive through the stories and reflections of popular author Megan McKenna. Her words show us how we can center our lives on bringing justice and peace into the world while we wait for Jesus, the Son of God, to come among us. This volume includes the four Sunday readings in Advent Cycles A, B and C, as well as the feasts of the Immaculate Conception, Our Lady of Guadalupe, the three Christmas Masses, the Holy Family, and Epiphany.

978-1-56548-300-2
256 pp., paperback

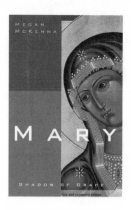

Mary

Shadow of Grace
(New & expanded edition)

"A study of the life of the Blessed Mother from a lay woman with extraordinary writing ability is a real treat. A most refreshing book."

Our Sunday Visitor

"McKenna is a storyteller with a passion for justice, and this book is marvelous prose. It is an excellent choice for reflection on Marian celebrations throughout the church year."

National Catholic Reporter

ISBN 978-1-56548-260-9
192 pp., paperback

Mother to All, Mother Forever

Four Weeks with Mary of Nazareth

Pope John Paul II referred to Mary as Mother to all, and Mother forever. The faithful know they can count on the heavenly Mother's concern: Mary will never abandon them. By taking her into our own home as a supreme gift from the heart of the crucified Christ, we are assured a uniquely effective presence in the task of showing the world in every circumstance the fruitfulness of love and the authentic meaning of life.

ISBN 978-1-56548-316-3
72 pp., paperback

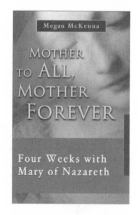